The GREAT DEPRESSION *for* KIDS

The GREAT DEPRESSION *for* KIDS

HARDSHIP AND HOPE IN 1930S AMERICA ❧ with 21 Activities

Cheryl Mullenbach

CHICAGO REVIEW PRESS

© 2015 by Cheryl Mullenbach
All rights reserved
First edition
Published by Chicago Review Press, Incorporated
814 North Franklin Street
Chicago, Illinois 60610
ISBN 978-1-61373-051-5

Library of Congress Cataloging-in-Publication Data
Is available from the Library of Congress.

Cover and interior design: Monica Baziuk
Cover images: Front cover images (clockwise from top left): Shirley Temple, Photofest; "A good lunch," Library of Congress LC-USZC2-5427; Franklin Delano Roosevelt, Library of Congress LC-USZ62-32833; Marcus Garvey, Library of Congress LC-USZ61-1854; migrant girl, Library of Congress LC-USF33-011985-M4; unemployed men sitting at the San Francisco Public Library, Library of Congress LC-DIG-fsa-8b31676; sharecropper's home, Library of Congress LC-DIG-fsa-8a16542. Back cover images (top to bottom): Herbert Hoover, Library of Congress LC-USZ62-131568; Zora Neale Hurston, Library of Congress LC-DIG-van-5a52142; children working in a potato field, Library of Congress LC-DIG-fsa-8a22232; pack horse librarian, National Archives (69-N-12581C)
Interior illustrations: James Spence

Printed in the United States of America
5 4 3 2 1

For Ralph and Zola

And always for Richard L. Wohlgamuth

CONTENTS

ACKNOWLEDGMENTS

Thanks to my editor at Chicago Review Press, Lisa Reardon. My gratitude to Bruce R. Fehn for his insight and expertise as a historian. Thank you to the Miller family—Jeff, Kristie, Bailey, Zack, and Brooklyn—for help in developing and testing the activities.

TIME LINE

1934 National Industrial Recovery Act guarantees
workers the right to form unions

1935 Social Security Act signed

George Gallup begins polling Americans

Emergency Relief Appropriation Act
provides funds for public works projects

National Youth Administration provides
jobs and training for young people

Works Progress Administration establishes
Federal Art Project, Federal Music Project, Federal
Writers' Project, Federal Theatre Project

1936 Workers in Michigan stage sit-down strike

Dorothea Lange captures image of *Migrant Mother*

First National Football League draft is held

1937 Amelia Earhart disappears in the Pacific Ocean

Joe Louis captures heavyweight
champion of the world title

1938 Fair Labor Standards Act of 1938
limits work for kids under 16

Second Agricultural Adjustment Act is passed,
helping small farmers and tenant farmers

Farm Security Administration created to help
migrant workers and farmers who rented land

Helen Wills Moody retires from tennis after
winning her eighth Wimbledon title

1939 World War II begins in Europe

Joe DiMaggio named baseball's
Most Valuable Player

THE MYSTERY *of the* MIGRANT FAMILY

Life as a migrant family in 1936 was harsh. The woman in the photo *Migrant Mother* (at right) and the two little girls knew just how tough it was. The baby would soon learn.

For over 40 years no one knew much about the family in the photo. It was taken by Dorothea Lange, who worked in a program that used photographs to tell the stories of migrant families—those who moved frequently from place to place to find temporary farming work.

Dorothea ran across this mother and her children at a camp in California. They lived in a tent. Other migrant families lived in the camp. They took jobs working in the farm fields. The nearby fields of peas had been destroyed by cold weather. Most workers were moving on to the next place where they hoped to find work.

The mother in the photo was a widow, and her car had broken down. She couldn't go anywhere. She and her children were eating the frozen peas from the fields, and birds that her older children had caught.

Before Dorothea captured the photo she promised the woman she would never tell anyone her name. In fact, Dorothea never asked for it.

The day after the photo was taken, newspapers around the country published it. Many Americans were shocked by the image of the woman and her children. They were disturbed to hear about conditions in the camp.

Long after the Great Depression ended, this image of the migrant mother and her children symbolized the hopelessness of the time. School textbooks tried to describe the era. People who lived through it struggled to explain their feelings. But all anyone has to do is look at the face of the mother in the photograph to understand what it must have been like for many Americans during this dark time.

The names of the woman and her children remained a mystery. But the emotions visible in the mother's face and the shame expressed by her children, who hid their faces from the camera, were not unknown to many people who lived during the Great Depression. While shame and despair were widespread during those troubling times, many people who lived through the Great Depression recall other, more positive memories—acts of courage, pride, and generosity shown by countless individuals and agencies. Some of those stories—of hardship *and* hope— are told in *The Great Depression for Kids*.

The *Migrant Mother* and her children.

Courtesy of the Library of Congress, Prints & Photographs Division, FSA/OWI Collection, LC-DIG-fsa-8b29516

Robert Jones.

THE 1920s: ROARING TOWARD *a* CRASH

Robert Tyre Jones Jr. was competing for a national golf championship when he hit his golf ball into the woods. He followed the ball into the secluded area and accidentally touched it—an act that would result in a penalty that could hurt his chances of moving into first place in the tournament. Robert was alone in the woods, and no one would ever have known that he committed the error. In that moment, he made a difficult decision. When he returned to the main course, he reported his actions—resulting in a one-stroke penalty. It was enough to cost him the championship.

The 1920s were a time of contrasts. Admirable men like Robert Tyre Jones Jr. shared the spotlight with notorious gangsters such as Al Capone. Bold businesspeople made millions buying and selling stocks, while farmers struggled to feed their families. Mothers—who concealed their legs in yards of heavy skirts and constrained their waist-length hair into tight buns—clashed with daughters, who exposed not only ankles but knees too and shed their long locks for bobbed hair.

The decade of the 1920s was known by different names—the Roaring Twenties, the Incredible Era, and the Era of Excess. Those labels make the 1920s sound like a very good time. But it's important to remember that people and events in the Roaring Twenties contributed to the future decade of misery known as the Great Depression.

Men and women who worked in the factories, bought their first cars, and listened to baseball games on their new radios had no idea that the Roaring Twenties would come to a crashing halt. Young women who danced the Charleston and men who had seen the sights of Paris during World War I could not imagine that their futures held anything but a roaring good time.

GOOD RIDDANCE to 1919

ALL ACROSS the country merrymakers were celebrating. It was December 31, 1919—New Year's Eve. In some ways it was like any New Year's in the past—revelers in fine clothes sharing a special night with friends and family. But it was unlike others too. Americans were especially eager to see the old year—and the old decade—pass. The previous years had been rough.

The nation had been divided over issues including the drinking of alcohol and voting by women. When the 18th Amendment to the Constitution was passed outlawing the manufacture and sale of alcoholic beverages, some people were overjoyed, but others were dismayed. As men and women petitioned for laws allowing women to vote, citizens debated the wisdom of this move.

The world would never be the same after the brutal conflict that became known as the Great War. Millions of lives had been lost. A worldwide influenza epidemic—called a pandemic—caused 50 million deaths.

Many were ready to ring in a new year that they hoped would signal an era of good fortune.

LIFE WITHOUT WAR

THE GREAT War ended in November 1918. It had affected the world in many ways. Lives had been lost, cities damaged, businesses disrupted. Food was scarce for some.

America entered the war in 1917, but other countries had begun fighting in 1914. The war affected the US economy. Factories churned out military equipment, uniforms, and guns. Banks lent money to warring governments. Farmers in war-torn countries could not plant and harvest crops, so American farmers had become responsible for feeding the world. The

Great War had helped the American economy boom.

When the Great War came to an end in late 1918, it affected the economy worldwide. European nations were in bad shape because the war had been fought there. European governments couldn't repay money they owed the United States. American factories didn't need to produce all those war materials now that the fighting was finished. They started to scale back. They needed fewer workers.

The first two years of the decade of the Roaring Twenties were not good for many. In general, the economy was sluggish. It was not "roaring." Most would say it was whimpering.

A SHAKY START to a NEW DECADE

SEVENTY FIVE BOYS were suspended from school in Eau Claire, Wisconsin, in April 1920. They had thrown two classmates into a lake because the two weren't wearing denim clothes. The boys were members of a movement that swept the nation early in 1920. Overall Clubs were springing up in schools, businesses, and colleges from Boston to Seattle.

They were protesting the high cost of clothing. Members of the clubs vowed to wear denim fabrics that were cheap and normally not worn in professional or social situations. Overall Club members advised, "Use up old clothing." And, most important, "Don't purchase high-priced slacks, shirts, and dresses."

The idea spread. In Missouri a minister pledged to wear overalls during services. In Washington students attended classes in old clothes made of khaki. Students in Lewiston, Idaho, claimed they had enrolled 200 members in their Overall Club.

The Overall Movement was big news for about 10 days. And while it may not have made a difference in clothing prices, it brought attention to a problem that affected many Americans in the early 1920s. High prices for goods would be an ongoing issue.

Eleven-year-old Hallie Underwood didn't know much about the economy in the early 1920s. But she knew her coal miner dad couldn't find work. Hallie lived with her parents and seven siblings in West Virginia.

The Underwoods were about to be evicted from their house. They had little food. They heated the house with coal that the kids picked up from scrap piles. Things looked bad for the Underwood family and many other miners' families.

Miners shared hard times with other wage earners, including textile, steel, and rail workers during the early 1920s. The unemployment rate in the United States was 11 percent. Thousands were out of work.

In Michigan eight-year-old Charles was in charge of his brothers and sister—ages five years to three months. He cooked the meals for the kids and packed lunch for his parents, who were picking beets in a nearby field. The family lived in a one-room shack with no windows.

Charles and his family were migrant workers in the Roaring Twenties. They moved from farm to farm harvesting crops for the farmers who owned the land. It was a tough life.

Farm families' lives were hard too during the Roaring Twenties. During the Great War, farmers produced food to feed the world. "Food will win the war" was a popular slogan farmers liked to boast. American farmers earned high prices for their products. They bought more land and equipment. Some borrowed money to purchase additional land.

When the war ended, farmers began to suffer. Soon there were surpluses of crops. It was a very bad time for farm families. And hard times continued throughout the 1920s. So when farmers talked about the Roaring Twenties, they saw it as a time to "roar" or complain—not a time to have a "roaring good time."

THE ROARING TWENTIES TAKE OFF

By 1922 the economy was beginning to turn around. For the first time in history, more Americans lived in cities than in rural areas. New products—radios, appliances, and automobiles—were being manufactured in record numbers. Advertising in magazines and newspapers and on the radio made consumers eager to purchase these items. People had money left over after they paid for the essentials. If they didn't have extra money, there was a new option available.

The installment plan was designed to let buyers take home their merchandise immediately and pay for it over time. Even houses were purchased on the installment plan—with mortgages through a bank. It was a new idea in the 1920s. It helped make the economy "roar." People began buying like crazy.

One man joked that his wife was headed to "make three back payments on the furniture, one back payment on the radio, part of a back payment on the rug." He was exaggerating, but getting behind on payments was no joke for many Americans. It became a real problem.

Something else began to make headlines. Stories circulated about hardworking, ordinary Americans investing in the stock market—buying shares of large corporations. And it sounded like quite a few people were becoming millionaires overnight!

There was a nurse who made $30,000 playing the stock market—a fortune to most Americans, who made around $2,000 a year. A valet was reported to have made a quarter million. People heard about these fabulous successes, and it made them believe that anyone could get rich.

Some of those investors bought stocks in a way that caused problems. They bought stocks on margin, which meant, for example, a buyer who wanted to buy a stock worth $1,000 paid $100 and borrowed the other $900. This was a risky move. If the stock increased in value, the buyer paid off his or her $900 loan and made money on top of it. However, if the stock decreased in value, the buyer couldn't repay the $900 loan. This practice of buying stocks on margin helped cause a disaster in the late 1920s.

TIME to CLOSE AMERICA'S GATES

"ANY CHANGE that will give us less immigration is to be desired. Our gates have stood open long enough." This was the opinion in 1924 of the commissioner of immigration at Ellis Island, the port of entry for many newcomers. This opinion was shared by many Americans in the 1920s. Congress passed laws that made sure the gates slammed shut on *some* immigrants.

Two immigration laws were passed in the 1920s that limited the number of immigrants who came to the United States. By 1927 only about 160,000 immigrants were allowed into the country each year. It wasn't so much the reduction in *numbers* of immigrants that was unfair. The acts discriminated according to ethnicity. People from southern and eastern Europe and from Asia were considered less desirable than immigrants from western and northern Europe. Immigration from Canada was not restricted.

The laws slowed down the arrival of new immigrants, but there were plenty already in the country. Some Americans decided to deal with immigrants in their own ways.

"...[Y]ou policemen may protect them, but we will get them sooner or later." In the summer of 1921 a newspaper reported this threat made by a resident of a Pennsylvania town. Residents had decided to drive out "undesirable foreigners," whom they blamed for crimes in the community.

In Indiana a group of citizens drove about 100 "foreigners" from their town. The immigrants had been hired by the local coal mine, and the resident miners said there were plenty of local men who should be hired instead.

Life for immigrants in the United States could be dangerous in the 1920s. Why did so many Americans fear and hate them? After all, many Americans had been immigrants at one time too.

Some of the fear was fueled by people called "nativists." They were people who were born in the United States—native born. They believed their religions, customs, and interests were more important than those of others. They feared that the ideas and cultures of immigrants would bring unwanted changes to the United States.

Some labor unions feared immigrants would take jobs away from American workers. Because immigrants were willing to accept lower wages, companies were willing to hire them.

Even government leaders expressed fear of immigrants. It wasn't enough that new laws were passed to keep newcomers out of the United States. Some officials were intent on getting rid of those who were already in the country.

THE RED SCARE

EVENTS IN a country far from the United States led Americans to fear immigrants. A revolution occurred in Russia in 1917. The czar, or king, was driven from power. The country was taken over by Communists—people who believed the government should have total control over the economy.

Communists were active in the United States at the same time. They were nicknamed "Reds." Some Communists had very frightening ideas. They thought violence and bombings were necessary to bring attention to their beliefs. Some Americans joined the Communists. They believed the only way to make life better was to overthrow the American government and set up a new economic system.

Government officials didn't like the sound of this. And neither did many Americans. It happened that some of the Communists were immigrants. That's all it took for some Americans to lump *all* immigrants into one category—Reds!

It was not against the law to be a Communist in America. However, it was a crime to use violence and to try to overthrow the government, so government leaders wanted to put an end to illegal activities by Communists.

In 1919 and 1920 Attorney General A. Mitchell Palmer was extremely active in trying to find Communists who were advocating the overthrow of the American way of life. Many immigrants were unjustly accused of illegal activity. Their civil rights were disregarded. Some were deported. This period became known as the Red Scare.

Some believed two Italian immigrants were victims of the Red Scare. Nicola Sacco and Bartolomeo Vanzetti were convicted of murder in Massachusetts in 1920. The evidence against them was weak. Their rights were violated during the trial, but they were found guilty and executed in 1927.

Sacco and Vanzetti were known to have radical ideas about the government. They both believed the Great War was unjust, so they refused to fight on the side of America. Although the two held radical opinions, there was little proof that they were murderers. There were many who believed they were unjustly convicted and executed.

OPPORTUNITIES, DISAPPOINTMENTS, HOPE for AFRICAN AMERICANS

EMILE TREVILLE Holley had been an outstanding high school student in Flushing, New York. He was a member of the dramatic club and a skilled athlete. His accomplishments and reputation in high school had helped him get into college. In the spring of 1922 Emile was only 17 years old and finishing his first year at the College of the City of New York.

While in college Emile was nominated to enter the US Naval Academy. And he was just the type of young man the US Naval Academy at Annapolis, Maryland, wanted in its ranks. So why did Emile's appointment cause such a stir?

It was newsworthy because Emile was African American. The *New York Times* reported that officials at the Naval Academy made it clear Emile would have a difficult time at Annapolis if he passed the entrance exam. The reporter who interviewed officers had "not talked to a single officer who does not deplore Holley as a candidate for Annapolis."

The navy never had to deal with the issue, because Emile didn't pass the entrance exam. Although a military career was not in Emile's future, he went on to finish college and became an English professor.

In some ways the Great War had created opportunities for black families. During the war business owners were desperate for workers. Many white men had left their jobs to join the military. So business owners went to southern states to hire black men to work in the northern cities. Families left their homes in the South for jobs in the northern factories.

Emile Holley with college friends.

© Bettmann/CORBIS

While this meant better wages, there was uncertainty too. Many who moved knew business owners might apply the "last hired, first fired" policy after the war. Black men who had been hired could be fired when the white men returned. Many of those African Americans who were hired for war jobs *were* fired. In some cases, it was because there were fewer jobs after the war. In some situations they were fired so that white men could have the jobs.

Over 350,000 African American men had served in the military during the Great War in segregated units. They were hopeful that their service would change the way white Americans treated them. They thought they might be welcomed home as heroes and that job opportunities would await them. This was not the case. Little changed in terms of civil rights for black Americans during the 1920s.

The 1920s brought about the rebirth of a hate group—the Ku Klux Klan (KKK). This secret society was a danger to immigrants, Catholics, Jews, and African Americans. It became more powerful in the 1920s after being quiet for a few years. The size of the Klan increased. And its violent activities were renewed.

In 1900, 90 percent of African Americans had lived in the southern United States. This changed drastically at the time of the Great War, when African Americans left the South for northern states. The black populations of northern and western cities grew by about 40 percent between 1910 and 1930. This mass movement became known as the Great Migration.

Odette Harper didn't know anything about a Great Migration when she played a game called jacks on the sidewalk in her Harlem, New York, neighborhood in the 1920s. The game required players to toss a little ball in the air and scoop up jacks while the ball was in motion. It was not all that easy for a 10-year-old. But Odette had fun trying.

A man named Marcus Garvey lived on Odette's street. She knew he was someone of great importance to the black community. Most adults treated him with respect. So the kids in the neighborhood knew they should be polite to him.

Marcus often visited with the kids as they played in the streets. He liked to join Odette in the game of jacks. He was a very skilled competitor. The kids were nice to Marcus, but they were always happy to see him leave.

"I liked him okay. But I wanted him to go away. He was just too good at jacks," Odette said.

Marcus was a well-known African American figure. He had started a group called the Universal Negro Improvement Association (UNIA) in 1914. Branches were formed around the United States. Through the association Marcus inspired self-reliance and equality for African Americans. He encouraged them to cherish their culture and heritage.

In the 1920s Marcus started to ask black Americans to consider leaving the United States. He believed equality was not possible in America. He talked about starting a new nation in Africa. Marcus called it the Back-to-Africa movement.

Marcus's dreams for a better world for African Americans were hurt when he was found guilty of fraud related to the UNIA. He was deported to the land of his birth—Jamaica, British West Indies. He never returned to the United States. But Marcus Garvey's influence lived on as many Americans followed his advice to value their African backgrounds.

During the 1920s Harlem, a neighborhood in New York, began to flourish because it was home to many talented black artists, writers, and performers. Some had come to the area as part of the Great Migration. Others had lived there for generations. In Harlem, African Americans felt free to express themselves through the arts and music. They showed pride in their culture. They became successful as entrepreneurs.

This period of great growth and thriving activity in the area was called the Harlem Renaissance. It was as though many African Americans were awakening to a new life—with opportunities and hope for a better future. It was a "roaring" time for the economy and the arts in Harlem.

Gwen Knight was 13 years old when she moved to Harlem in 1926. It was a momentous move for her. She spent her teen years amid the rich cultural environment of Harlem, where she was in close contact with artists and musicians who inspired her love of dance, theater, and opera. Gwen's early years in Harlem led her to a lifetime of painting. When she died at the age of 92 in 2005, she was a renowned artist.

Marcus Garvey.
Courtesy of the Library of Congress, Prints & Photographs Division, LC-USZ61-1854

When Zora Neale Hurston was 13, her mother died. It was her mother's encouragement to "jump at the sun" that shaped Zora's life. By the time she was 14 her father had remarried, to a woman whom Zora didn't like. So she left home and settled in Maryland, where she attended high school and college. During the 1920s she began to write for African American publications in Harlem. Throughout the 1920s and '30s Zora became a respected author of novels, poems, and nonfiction—including *Their Eyes Were Watching God*, "O Night," and "The Ten Commandments of Charm."

Marcus Garvey, Gwen Knight, and Zora Neale Hurston were just three of many African Americans who blossomed during the glory days of the Harlem Renaissance. Disappointments brought on by racism and discrimination were somewhat softened by the opportunities and hope that the Harlem Renaissance spawned.

A ROARING GOOD TIME

"How 'Ya Gonna Keep 'Em Down on the Farm After They've Seen Paree?"

IT WAS a popular song written in 1918 by Joe Young and Sam M. Lewis. They were trying to make a point about returning veterans who had seen the sights of Europe—especially Paris, France. Many were young men who were raised in small towns or on farms. The people, entertainments, and customs of European cities such as Paris were very different—and exciting—for these American boys.

In the decade after the Great War, Americans witnessed great changes in the way people

Zora Neale Hurston.

thought and acted. Young people, some of whom had experienced unimaginable events in Europe—both horrifying *and* fascinating—viewed their world differently than their parents. They expressed their ideas through their dress, behavior, art, literature, and music. The new ideas of the young sometimes clashed with the beliefs of the older generation.

One of the most visible changes during the Roaring Twenties was the way men and women dressed and wore their hair. Young men began to shed beards. Slicked-down hair parted in the middle or slightly off to one side was stylish.

Young men in the 1920s wore lighter-colored clothes than their dads. Suspenders were replaced by belts. Pants had crisp creases down the front of the legs. Dress shoes were two-toned. Men wore hats with one side of the brim up and the other side down. Leather aviator jackets were the rage.

College boys wore long raccoon coats to show off their wealth. But the coats were practical too. They kept riders warm in the open-topped automobiles of the 1920s, and spectators cozy at football games. They topped off the flashy coats with straw hats called boaters.

Young women rejected the ankle-length skirts of their mothers. Short, colorful dresses that showed the calves were popular. Girls rolled their long stockings down to expose bare knees. They shed confining corsets, colored their cheeks with rouge, and applied bright lipstick. They cut their hair into short, sassy bobs.

The image of a woman dressed in the new styles, dancing up a storm, and adopting the new attitudes about behavior became a symbol for the new modern roles for women. Women of the Roaring Twenties were encouraged to be confident and independent. They dressed differently than their mothers. And they acted differently. Those who fit this description were known as flappers.

Young women cut their hair and shortened their skirts.

Courtesy of the Library of Congress, Prints & Photographs Division, LC-USZ62-42063

The changes in styles were outward symbols of what was happening in society—especially with women. Many were feeling free from their old roles. Women had contributed to the war effort in factories, on farms, and on the battlefield as military personnel and nurses. Electric appli- ances relieved women of unpleasant duties in their homes. Automobiles were becoming common. Women had opportunities to step out with men—unchaperoned. Women began to drive themselves.

More women (and men) graduated high school and college. Women pursued careers and work outside the home. They could vote thanks to the passage of the 19th Amendment to the Constitution in 1919. They became involved in politics. Girls were introduced to successful, professional women through newspapers, radio, and movies. These changes resulted in a label for those who looked for a different way of life from their mothers—the "New Woman."

Young men and women took pleasure in the freedoms of the Roaring Twenties. African Americans brought the sounds of jazz to the northern states; both blacks and whites appreciated musicians like Louis Armstrong and Duke Ellington. Jazz became so much a part of the 1920s that the era was called the Jazz Age.

New fast-paced, energetic dance forms became popular. The Charleston, Lindy Hop, and Shimmy were the craze. Magazines published photos showing step-by-step moves. People watched stars performing the steps in movies and copied them at local dance halls.

Dance marathons became the rage. Couples or individuals competed to see who could keep moving on the dance floor the longest. Prize

CORSET QUEEN SURVIVES THE ROARING TWENTIES

MADAME ROSA BINNER started her career in corsets when she was only 11 years old. In the 1880s she worked as an assistant to a European corset maker. In 1896 Rosa moved to America.

At first Rosa struggled. She spoke not a word of English. It was a few weeks before she realized she was actually living in Hoboken, New Jersey. She thought she was in New York City!

When she did finally get settled in an apartment in New York, she began making corsets. Her first customers were maids. When their wealthy employers discovered that their maids' trim figures were formed by Rosa's corsets, they wanted them too.

Rosa's business grew. She began making corsets for some of America's most celebrated entertainers–opera singers, performers, and movie stars.

During the 1920s when young women rejected the wearing of corsets, many corset manufacturers went out of business. Not Madame Binner. She started making lighter-weight silk styles to make flappers and adventurous women happy.

"Now the girls are flying [airplanes]. They must adapt their corsets to the air. Their corsets must expand as the flyers change positions–or make parachute jumps," she explained.

Madame Binner designed a corset for glamorous film star Lillian Russell. The $3,900 satin garment was decorated with diamonds. The star was so thrilled with her undergarment that when her house caught fire, she reportedly shouted to the firefighters, "Never mind my jewels. Rescue my corset!"

money was at stake so judges prowled the dance floor to determine that couples were dancing. They expected to see feet moving up and down. Knees touching the floor meant disqualification. When one partner got so tired he or she had to sleep, the other propped up the sleeper while continuing to move across the dance floor. The last couple standing won the prize money.

While many Americans were dismayed with the new uninhibited dance forms like the Charleston and the Shimmy, others turned their attention to the religious rituals of Native Americans. INDIANS' DANCES SHOCK MORALS OF MR. BURKE, read one newspaper headline in 1921 describing the reaction of the federal government's commissioner of Indian affairs to a religious dance. Under Charles Burke's guidance, the federal government issued directives that outlined the "degrading" and "harmful" nature of certain dances conducted by some Native Americans. But the Native Americans disagreed. They said their customs were sacred, and there was nothing immoral about their religions.

Alcoholic beverages had been part of social activities before the passage of the 18th Amendment, which outlawed the sale of alcohol beginning in 1919. The following period of time was called Prohibition. All through the 1920s it was against the law for public places to sell alcoholic drinks. Many people thought this was a good

Law enforcement officers pour illegal alcohol down the street sewer. Courtesy of the Library of Congress, Prints & Photographs Division, LC-USZ62-123257

decision. Others disagreed. Plenty of Americans decided they would get alcohol one way or another—despite the law.

For those who wanted to drink, there were places called speakeasies. These were bars that secretly sold alcohol. The police often raided the speakeasies hoping to find illegal activity. Oftentimes the owners were warned by local law enforcement officials who were friends of business owners that a raid was scheduled, and they would quickly hide their alcohol.

Despite the law, the alcohol business continued in secret. Bootleggers made alcohol or transported it from other countries where it was legal. Gangs of bootleggers created networks that made it quite easy for people to get alcohol.

Al Capone was one of the most famous gangsters of the era. He violated all the elements of the law that outlawed alcohol. He manufactured, imported, and sold it. He and his accomplices led violent and dangerous lives. While Americans feared gangsters like Al Capone, they also were fascinated by them.

Changes in transportation greatly affected Americans in the 1920s. Automobiles changed the way people lived, worked, and played. In 1919 there were only 7 million cars in the country. By 1929 there were over 23 million! Large numbers of people owned cars because the prices had dropped considerably. In 1914 a Ford car cost $850. By 1926 the cost was $350.

The airplane industry was in its infancy. Planes had been used by the military to win the Great War. In the 1920s planes were used commercially to transport cargo and passengers. Charles Lindbergh became a celebrity for his flying feats. In 1927 he completed the first nonstop solo flight across the Atlantic Ocean. In 1927 the "Flying Flapper," Ruth Elder, hoped to become the first woman to cross the Atlantic in her plane, *American Girl*. However, Ruth and her copilot, George Haldeman, had to ditch over water near the Azores when the plane malfunctioned. Bessie Coleman, the first African American female pilot, brought attention to airplanes through her performances in air shows.

Throughout the decade of the Roaring Twenties, there was plenty to roar about. Americans followed the exploits of gangsters and airplane stunt performers, bought tickets to dance marathons and movies, took vacations with their new automobiles, gained citizenship and listened to jazz. There were struggles—layoffs, wage reductions, unemployment, high prices, rent increases, and deportations. But in general, life in America was quite agreeable during the 1920s.

THE ROAR ENDS with a CRASH

By the end of the decade some disturbing economic news was beginning to surface. In the summer of 1929, spending by consumers was falling. Americans were buying fewer cars and houses. Businesses were cutting production of goods. But it was the fall of 1929 that brought very troubling events.

That fall, things began to get very shaky with the stock market. Prices began to drop. Investors began to sell their shares quickly. The value

Ruth Elder and George Haldeman aboard a ship after their failed flight across the Atlantic.
National Air and Space Museum (NASM A-5211), Smithsonian Institution

INVESTIGATE THE SCIENCE OF PAPER AIRPLANES

THE AGE OF FLIGHT was just taking off in the 1920s. The only airplane the average citizen would have flown at that time would have been one made of paper! Paper airplanes use some of the same science as real planes—including physics. By adjusting the weight of paper used in your airplane you will influence the distance your planes can fly.

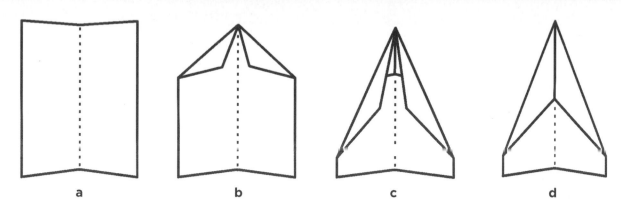

a   b   c   d

You'll Need

- 1 sheet 8½ by 11-inch (216 by 279-millimeter) printer paper
- 1 sheet 8½ by 11-inch (216 by 279-millimeter) construction paper
- 1 piece 8½ by 11-inch (216 by 279-millimeter) posterboard
- Duct tape or chalk
- Tape measure
- Pencil and notepad

1. Fold all three pieces of paper into the airplane shape:

a. Fold paper in half lengthwise (figure a).

b. Fold each corner at one end to form triangles (figure b).

c. Fold triangles to meet in the middle of the plane (figure c).

d. Fold the middle of paper in half where the original fold was made.

e. Fold both "wings" down as shown (figure d).

2. Go to a location where you can test the distance of the planes' flights. It should be a wide open space.

3. Tape a line on the ground, or draw a line with chalk. This is where you will stand to throw your plane. It's important that you stand in the same spot each time so that your measurements are consistent.

4. Throw the paper plane five times. Record the distance for each flight.

5. Repeat for the construction paper plane and the posterboard plane.

6. Average the distances for each plane. (Add up the distances, then divide by 5.)

7. Use the average to record the planes' flight distance.

8. Ask yourself which plane flew the greatest distance?

PLAY THE STOCK MARKET

ONE CAUSE of the stock market crash in 1929 was reckless stock buying. People borrowed money to invest in stocks, but when the market crashed they were left with worthless investments. Then they couldn't repay the money they had borrowed. In this activity you will use an imaginary gift of $10,000 to purchase stocks. Buy and sell wisely!

You'll Need
- ✈ **Computer with Internet access or daily newspaper**
- ✈ **Calculator**
- ✈ **Paper and pen**

Go online or read the newspaper and identify some companies that are on the New York Stock Exchange. Choose one or more that you would like to invest in. You can use this website to find companies: www.nyse.com/about/listed/lc_all_overview.html.

An example of an imaginary stock is shown in the chart. Track your *real* stock's actual activity by completing the form.

Name of stock	Pretend Stock	
Date of purchase	January 10, 2014	
Purchase price	$50 per share	
Number of shares purchased	100	
Total money spent (purchase price × number of shares purchased)	100 × 50 = $5,000	
Dividend per share (Some stocks pay a dividend—or periodic payment—to shareholders.)	Jan to Mar = 15 cents Apr to June = 20 cents July to Sept = 10 cents Sept to Dec = 10 cents	
Total amount made on each dividend (dividend per share × number of shares purchased)	Jan to Mar 100 × .15 = $15 Apr to June 100 × .20 = $20 July to Sept 100 × .10 = $10 Sept to Dec 100 × .10 = $10 Total = $55	
Date sold	January 10, 2015	
Price when sold	$60	
Total money made or lost on sale	Dividends = $55 Sale = $1,000 Total = $1,055	

Adapted with permission from a lesson developed by Alan Niceswanger, Prairie Valley Community Schools, Gowrie, Iowa.

of many stocks kept dropping. On October 29, 1929, 16 million shares of stock were sold. That was about three times the usual amount for a day. It caused widespread loss of money for some Americans. It became known as the "crash" of the stock market.

The crash was crushing to those who had put their life savings into stocks. It was a blow to wealthy investors who lost millions but still had millions. Most Americans had not invested in the stock market in the 1920s. So for most Americans October 30—the day after the crash—was like any other. Newspaper headlines covered a variety of events:

CLOSING OF WEST VIRGINIA FOOTBALL CONTEST COMPLETES SCHEDULE

BALTIMORE TO FORM NEGRO ORCHESTRA

CANADIAN COUPLE, 103 AND 93, HOLD 74TH WEDDING ANNIVERSARY

TIME TO BUY STOCKS, SEES ONLY TEMPORARY EFFECT ON BUSINESS

The headlines were deceiving. While people did continue to cheer their sports teams, play in orchestras, and celebrate life's big events, the crash of the stock market was a significant event that was a sign of very unstable economic conditions. And soon most Americans would feel the effects of the ailing economy. But on October 30, 1929, no one could know that. People didn't realize just how bad things could get. They would soon find out.

TEENS COMPETE IN MARYLAND

WHEN HISTORIANS LOOKED BACK to the summer of 1929, they saw signs that the American economy was heading toward a crash. When William Ruppert and Dorothy Staylor looked back to that summer, they remembered one of the most memorable of their lives.

It was the summer that a man named Alvin "Shipwreck" Kelly had come to their hometown of Baltimore, Maryland, to demonstrate a fad that had swept the country. Shipwreck had become a sensation for setting records for flagpole sitting. In 1924 Shipwreck had perched for 13 hours and 13 minutes atop a flagpole. That got him a lot of attention and started a fad that attracted other daredevils. Everybody wanted to break the latest flagpole-sitting record.

After Shipwreck visited Baltimore and broke another record for *adult* flagpole sitters, a bunch of kids were inspired to set a record for *juvenile* flagpole sitting.

A 15-year-old named Avon "Azie" Foreman declared himself the juvenile flagpole champion after 10 days, 10 hours, and 10 minutes on a pole. But there were other Baltimore kids who were ready to break Azie's record almost as soon as he climbed down from his perch.

Dorothy Staylor was criticized by the mother of a competitor when she mounted a 17-foot pole armed with pillows, a blanket, a silk scarf, an umbrella, a radio, and a library book. The mother accused Dorothy of competing from a "divan 15 feet in the air."

Paperboy William Ruppert was determined to break Azie's—as well as Shipwreck's—records. After 23 days the 14-year-old claimed to have done just that, and he planned to stay another 30 days. His friends complained because he wouldn't come down to swim or deliver his papers, but he did stay over 50 days on his pole, wearing out three pairs of trousers as he scooted about his suspended platform.

William Ruppert atop a flagpole. Library of Congress Prints and Photographs Division, LC-DIG-hec-35521

President Herbert and Mrs. Lou Henry Hoover.
Courtesy of the Library of Congress, Prints & Photographs Division, LC-USZ62-131568

AMERICA LOOKS *to* ITS LEADERS *for* HELP

Bert Hoover was a shy boy who liked to swim, hike, and explore around his small town of West Branch, Iowa, in the 1880s. In winter he enjoyed sledding, and in summer he could be found hunting fossils in fields or searching for colorful rocks along the railroad tracks. It was a very pleasant way of life for a kid. But it didn't last long. When Bert was six his dad died; only three years later his mom was dead too. Bert was an orphan at the age of nine.

Forty-four years later, in 1928, Americans went to the polls to cast their votes for president. Over 22 million—58 percent—of those who voted chose the candidate named Herbert Clark Hoover. The shy orphan boy known as Bert had become the 31st president of the United States.

In 1928 Herbert Hoover was so popular because Americans knew his remarkable story: he was an orphan who grew up to work his way through college and became an expert in mining operations, a very successful business owner, and eventually an extremely wealthy man. Many Americans were proud of the work he had done during the Great War when he set up a commission to get food to starving Europeans. He was also admired because when he was secretary of commerce he organized efforts to house and feed victims of the Mississippi River flood in 1927. People around the world called Herbert Hoover the Great Humanitarian.

The great respect and admiration Americans felt for Herbert Hoover did not last. When the stock market crashed in 1929, Americans looked to their president for leadership. As conditions grew worse in 1930—with many workers unemployed—people wanted intervention from their president. When families needed food and clothing, they expected help from the man known as the Great Humanitarian. But the president didn't seem to hear the calls for help from his fellow Americans.

HUNGRY AMERICANS LOOK to THEIR GOVERNMENT

AMERICA IN 1929 was very different than today. There were very few government programs to help old, sick, hungry, or unemployed people. It was up to family members, churches, or private charities to care for those who couldn't care for themselves.

As more and more Americans lost their jobs during the Great Depression, they looked to their government leaders for relief. But some of those leaders—including the president—had strong opinions about how to help suffering Americans.

Many government leaders and wealthy business owners were convinced that the government should not give food, clothing, or money to citizens. They believed that doing so would only make things worse. They thought if poor people just worked harder they would do better. They said if unemployed people were given money, they would never look for work.

President Hoover donated his salary to people affected by the Depression—$25,000 per year. But he was constantly criticized for ignoring the problems of ordinary Americans. The president believed it was not the responsibility of the federal government to give money to individuals. He said local governments and private groups should help unfortunate Americans.

President Hoover believed the federal government needed to help banks and large businesses such as railroads become stronger. If they did well, ordinary people would have jobs and do better too. He proposed an agency called the

Reconstruction Finance Corporation (RFC). It gave government loans to big companies and banks. But businesses and banks continued to shut down.

The nation's banks certainly needed help. Many had invested their depositors' money in the stock market. When it crashed in October 1929, many banks lost millions of dollars. In addition, banks had lent money to farmers, and farmers suffering from the hard economic conditions couldn't repay their loans. Banks—like other businesses during the Great Depression—were failing and shutting down. That meant people who thought they had money in accounts at these banks had nothing.

President Hoover's decisions to help banks and businesses left many people asking the question, "What about us?" It seemed the average American was being overlooked.

BONUS ARMY DEMANDS PAYMENT

AMONG THOSE overlooked Americans were veterans and their families. In the summer of 1932, news stories claimed a young boy was partially blinded. Two-year-old Raymond Hauser and 18-month-old Janet Reamer suffered from dysentery. Catherine Belt contracted typhoid. Two-month-old Bernard Myers died from exposure to tear gas. These

THE HOOVER NAME

AS THE GREAT DEPRESSION DEEPENED and more people suffered, the president became the target of Americans' discontent. Many couldn't think of anything positive to say about the president. They forgot that President Hoover had been a key person in the building of a magnificent dam on the Colorado River.

Early in the 1920s Herbert Hoover was secretary of commerce. He was admired for his skills in helping to determine how water would be distributed to the states surrounding the proposed dam. Seven states were affected. And because of Hoover's negotiation abilities and his engineering knowledge, a resolution was found.

Construction would take years to complete. By the time Hoover became president in 1928, the project was still in the planning stages. President Hoover pushed for the building to begin. He knew it was important for the economy because many workers would be employed by the project for several years.

Finally, in 1930 the work began on what was called the Boulder Dam project. Soon after the start, an official in the Hoover administration named it Hoover Dam. The name changed again later when Franklin Roosevelt became president and it became Boulder Dam. Finally, in 1947 it became Hoover Dam again and the name stuck.

Other "Hoover names" to come out of the Depression years include:

Hoover bags: Sacks carried by unemployed workers

Hoover hogs: Jackrabbits that farmers caught for food

Hoover blankets: Newspapers used by homeless people to keep warm

President Hoover may not have liked these terms, but he was very proud to have one of the world's greatest manmade structures named Hoover.

Hoover Dam. Courtesy of the Library of Congress, Prints & Photographs Division, LC-DIG-hec-14559

GIVE A HELPING HAND

AMERICANS LOOKED to their leaders for a helping hand during the early days of the Great Depression. However, it was usually private agencies such as the Red Cross, the Salvation Army, or Goodwill that provided food, clothing, and household items to people in need. All of these organizations and many others like them still exist. Make a plan to organize a collection drive for items needed by a charitable group of your choice. For example, an animal shelter may have a "wish list" of needed animal care supplies or general office supplies. A literacy program or organization may request specific types of books.

1. Contact your city government or Chamber of Commerce, or search online for a list of charitable organizations in your community.

2. Choose an organization that you'd like to help. Visit or call the organization and ask to meet with the person in charge of contributions. Explain that you want to organize a drive to gather items for the organization.

3. Ask the person you meet with what items the organization needs most. Ask for any other guidelines the group has for accepting contributions.

4. When you return home, make a detailed plan of action. Give your event a catchy name—like "Helping Hands." Develop a logo that represents your efforts. Use this form:

5. After you have completed the plan, contact friends and family (the "who" in the plan) and inform them of your activity. Ask if they can participate. Tell them the plan and discuss how to implement it. At this point, and actually at any point during the process, go back to the plan and revise if necessary.

6. Hold the event.

7. After the event, go back to your plan and make notes about how it went and what you would do differently next time.

Action Plan for Helping Hands:

a. Design logo

b. Who? (Helpers, your intended recipients, key people at the charitable organization, etc.)

c. What? (What is the event?)

d. When? (Is this a one-day event, or will it span several weeks?)

e. Where? (Will it include drop boxes at various locations? Or if it is a one-day event, where will it take place and at what time?)

f. Why? (Who will benefit?)

g. How? (This is where you need to think about exactly how you will implement this plan. Provide as much detail as possible. For example, if it is a one-day event, specify the schedule hour by hour.)

h. Promotion (How will people know about this? Posters? Local media? Social media? Etc.)

were children of men who had served in the Great War in 1918. They were living with their parents in camps near the grounds of the US Capitol in Washington, DC, and living conditions were very bad. The families had traveled to the nation's capital to demand the government pay the bonuses that had been promised to veterans after the Great War.

Every veteran who had served overseas was promised $1.25 plus interest for each day of service. That meant the average bonus would be about $1,000 for each veteran. It seemed like a fortune in 1932 when the country was deep into the Great Depression.

The government had originally ordered the payments for 1945—years in the future. But the

Bonus Army families lived in camps in Washington, DC.

BONUS MARCHING PETS

HOOVER THE GOAT; Patman the burro; Kazan the fire-eating dog. And an unnamed bunny.

Many of the bonus marchers brought their families with them to Washington, DC—wives, children, *and* pets.

One group of veterans traveled to the capital with Hoover the goat—named for the president. It was not meant to be a compliment to President Hoover, whom many Americans accused of being as stubborn as a goat when he refused to support the bonus marchers' cause.

A burro named Patman traveled from Texas. He was named after John William Wright Patman, the congressman who introduced a bill to pay the bonus marchers immediately. Patman the burro was a hit in Congressman Patman's office, where he performed tricks for the staff.

Another band of bonus marchers came up with a creative way to earn money for food along the way. They traveled with a dog named Kazan. He earned money by performing tricks in towns that the veterans passed through. Citizens of Hutchinson, Kansas, claimed Kazan ate fire in their town, and people paid to see it.

Seven-year-old Eugene King, the son of a veteran, had brought his pet rabbit along on the march. The King family lived in a tent in one of the camps. When the army was ordered to clear out the camp, one of the infantrymen came upon Eugene and reportedly shouted, "Get out of here, you little devil!" As the boy ran to the family's tent to get his pet, the soldier plunged his bayonet into Eugene's leg. Eugene recovered. The rabbit's fate was not reported.

veterans and their families were suffering greatly from the Great Depression. They were desperate. They didn't want to wait for 1945. They were hungry *now*.

In May a group started out from Oregon, led by an unemployed veteran named Walter Waters. The veterans hopped onto freight trains for their journey eastward to Washington to make their demands to President Hoover and Congress. As veterans in other cities and towns heard about the "bonus marchers," they also began to make their way to the nation's capital. They traveled by train, truck, car, and foot.

About 20,000 marchers descended on the city. They called themselves the Bonus Expeditionary Force (BEF). The veterans—and in some cases their families too—set up camps on vacant lots near government buildings. Congress refused to pass laws that would allow an earlier distribution of the bonus. And President Hoover refused to step in to help the veterans. He asked them to leave the city.

The BEF vowed to stay in Washington. They wanted to meet with President Hoover, and they wanted their bonuses. And as they waited, conditions in the makeshift camps got worse and worse. It was here that little Raymond, Janet, and Catherine got sick.

Finally, on July 28, government officials lost their patience. Washington's city police force was sent into the camp to evict the occupants. When one of the campers threw a brick at a policeman, the officers opened fire and killed two bonus marchers.

President Hoover sent in army troops, who used swords, tanks, and tear gas to drive out the families. When a soldier used his bayonet to jab an African American bonus marcher carrying an American flag, the veteran said, "Don't push me.

I fought for this flag. I fought in France, and I'm gonna fight for it here on Pennsylvania Avenue."

The flimsy structures in the camps—tents and shacks made of cardboard, burlap, and wood—caught fire. Hazy smoke and tear gas filled the air and made it difficult to breathe. The actions of the BEF and the government caused Americans to take notice. Many individuals and groups sent food and clothes to the camps for the marchers and their families.

But some people believed government officials who labeled the marchers as criminals and unpatriotic. Even President Hoover believed that some of the marchers were criminals. By late August the bonus marchers had gone back to their homes. They had not gotten their bonuses. They were angry, and President Hoover's image was badly tarnished because of his treatment of the veterans.

HUNGRY PEOPLE MARCH

Police Clubs Rout Hunger Marchers
Tear Gas Routs Hunger Marchers
Children March to Capitol

VETERANS WEREN'T the only ones demonstrating against the government. These headlines grabbed the attention of newspaper readers around the country during the 1930s. People were hungry, and they were desperate. Some

PREPARE DEPRESSION ERA SOUP

DURING THE WORST YEARS of the Depression, in the absence of government assistance, many hungry, out-of-work families depended on charity- or church-run soup kitchens for food. This soup recipe comes from the 1930s cookbook *Good Things to Eat*. Your soup will taste similar to those eaten in Depression Era soup kitchens. However, your experience will be quite different. Seconds are encouraged!

Adult supervision required

You'll Need
- 2 tablespoons butter or olive oil (called "fat" in the original recipe)
- 1 onion, sliced
- ½ to 1 cup water
- 1 carrot, diced
- 1 turnip, diced
- Pinch of minced parsley
- ½ stalk celery, diced
- 2 quarts beef stock (Today you can purchase cans or cartons of beef stock in a grocery store in the soup aisle. Do the math to decide how many cans/cartons you need. A 32-ounce carton equals 1 quart.)

1. Heat the butter/olive oil and the onion in a medium saucepan. Cook over medium heat until the onion is brown.

2. Add the water and stir with a wooden spoon.

3. Add the diced carrot, turnip, parsley, and celery and cook until tender.

4. Add the beef stock. Heat until very hot.

Serves 5

believed the only way to make President Hoover and other government leaders pay attention was to march to state capitals and in some cases occupy government buildings. Occasionally children marched with their parents.

In the fall of 1932 a group of about 30 children ranging in age from 2 to 15 years marched to the Michigan state capitol building. Along with an adult, the kids met with the governor and pre-

sented him with demands for food. The governor told them the state was "doing all in its power to bring relief."

"Heads bloody, marchers rolling on the pavement," the *Daily Boston Globe* reported conditions in Albany, New York, in October 1934. About 200 hunger marchers had tried to enter the city with demands for relief. Police armed with clubs formed a line across the Hudson River Bridge, preventing their approach. According to news reports, police picked up injured marchers and "tossed them in a wailing group at the side of the road."

In New Jersey, children played games in the aisles of the state legislature as their parents occupied the building. For nine days in May 1936 the hungry families refused to leave the statehouse. Finally, the weary protestors moved to the galleries as the legislators convened but failed to pass a relief measure. The families left peacefully, and the building was locked to prevent their return.

Another march of hungry people captured the attention of the country at Thanksgiving in 1932. Groups of marchers approached the White House and demanded a meeting with President Hoover. Police blocked the crowds and prevented them getting close to the president's house. Several marchers were arrested and taken to police headquarters.

Nothing was unusual about the arrest of hunger marchers. But at this Thanksgiving Day

Gertrude Haessler was arrested on Thanksgiving Day near the White House.

AP Photo

march on the White House 11-year-old Alice Mack of Philadelphia and 10-year-old Bernard Sales of New York City were among the marchers. The two, along with four other children, were detained by authorities. Arresting officers said they were just trying to protect the children. All were released by nightfall.

Some newspapers and many government leaders claimed that Communist agitators organized the hunger marches. They accused the Communists of trying to overthrow the government. Some of the marches *were* led by Communists. But others were organized by worried parents who didn't want their children to suffer.

LOOKING for a CHANGE in LEADERS

BY THE fall of 1932 many Americans saw nothing but problems in their country. The economy was in a shambles and the government—especially President Hoover—wasn't helping. When people were looking for someone to blame for the terrible situation, they looked at the president. The greatly admired man whom Americans had elected in 1928 had become the object of jokes. President Herbert Hoover was a very unpopular figure.

As the time to elect a president approached, some voters began to think about replacing President Hoover. They wanted a president who

INTERVIEW AN ELDER

MANY PEOPLE who can share memories of the 1930s are elderly today. It's important to learn about their experiences and feelings firsthand. Collect an oral history from a person who remembers life in the 1920s or '30s. With his or her permission, record the interview in audio and/or video. Create an end product that summarizes the information you learned from the interview. It could be a posterboard, a scrapbook, a video, a transcript, or another artifact. If the subject agrees, donate the artifact to a museum or library.

You'll Need
- Pad of paper
- Pen
- Interview questions
- Camera/video recorder

INTERVIEW QUESTIONS:
Name of interviewer
Date of interview
Name and address of subject
Where their ancestors lived
Place and date of birth
Immediate family
Education with dates and description of school days
Styles of clothing people wore—men, women, children
Favorite foods
Occupations and accomplishments, with dates
Special skills and interests
Community activities
Description of interviewee
Other points gained in interview

would offer a new way of handling the nation's huge problems.

When a man named Franklin Delano Roosevelt started talking about his plans for healing America if he were president, people began to notice. He talked about offering the country a "new deal."

"I pledge you, I pledge myself, a new deal for the American people," Franklin Roosevelt promised in a speech.

On November 8, 1932, voters cast their votes. Twenty-three million Americans chose the candidate who offered them a New Deal. Franklin Roosevelt would be the new president.

Franklin D. Roosevelt.
Courtesy of the Library of Congress, Prints & Photographs Division, LC-DIG-hec-47023

A NEW PRESIDENT,
a NEW DEAL

FROM THE minute Franklin Roosevelt took the oath of office for president, he began to explain in detail his New Deal for America. He tried to calm the fears that many had about the future. He used the radio to get his message into every home. His radio speeches were called *Fireside Chats*. His voice and his manner of speaking seemed friendly and reassuring.

In one of his *Fireside Chats* President Roosevelt outlined his New Deal. He explained that new government programs would help farmers, home owners, the unemployed, and needy families.

The president said, "We are encouraged to believe that a wise and sensible beginning has been made."

Maybe this "beginning" the new president mentioned would be the beginning of better times for everyone. If they could have seen into the future Americans would have seen that although the New Deal brought some relief, it truly was only a beginning. The end of hard times was years in the future.

Unemployed men gathered on the street in San Francisco, California, in 1937.

BROKEN CITIES *and* BREADLINES— URBAN LIFE

Twenty-year-old "Poison Ivy" King, decked out in a red satin cape, scarlet nail polish, and silver bracelets, was the darling of Roller Derby fans across America in the 1930s. White leather skates on her feet and big spectacles on her nose, she raced around tracks, leading her team of skaters to victory.

In the midst of the Great Depression, when many city dwellers faced broken services and streets overflowing with men in breadlines, Chicago businessman Leo Seltzer dreamed up a way to make some money for himself while bringing a new entertainment—Transcontinental Roller Derby—to cities across the country. Teams of skaters performed in major cities—Kansas City, Los Angeles, and New York City, among others.

Clarice Martin and Bernie McKay rolled to victory in the first Transcontinental Roller Derby.

At a time when many city dwellers were out of work and businesses had failed, Leo Seltzer and his skaters were doing quite well. Ivy earned $400 for a 25-day performance. Her paycheck was much appreciated in the King family. Ivy's unemployed dad had been getting "relief"—or government assistance—to support the family. With Ivy's help, the family was able to live without government aid.

The Transcontinental Roller Derby gave well-paying jobs to a few lucky skaters. More important, the exciting spectacles gave city dwellers a chance to think and talk about something other than their dreary lives in cities that were hard hit by the Great Depression.

MASSIVE UNEMPLOYMENT CRIPPLES FAMILIES

IVY KING'S family was one of millions who relied on relief to get through the darkest days of the Great Depression. After the stock market crashed in late 1929, things began to go downhill fast in America's cities and towns. Business activity slowed. People bought as little as possible. Businesses sold less merchandise. Factories produced fewer goods. So business owners and factories required fewer workers. Many lost their jobs, or their jobs were cut to part time.

Unemployment was a major problem in the 1930s. In 1929, before the stock market crash, 3 million Americans were unemployed. By 1932 the number of unemployed had leaped to 12.5 million. The average income for a family in 1929 was about $2,300. By 1933 it was $1,500.

Unemployment was a problem all over the country. People lost jobs in rural as well as urban areas. But it seemed more obvious in large cities. Many unemployed men wandered the streets. Some looked bedraggled. Others wore suits and hats. They were professionals as well as wage earners.

Job hunting became a way of life for many, but there were few opportunities. In Detroit men determined to be first in line waited all night outside a business where they heard jobs were available. A man in Arkansas walked 900 miles looking for work. In Manhattan an agency advertised 300 openings; 5,000 people applied.

In some large cities homeless people moved into shantytowns. These were structures built with scraps of lumber, tin, or cardboard. They had no electricity or running water. They provided shelter from the rain and snow but little else. While Herbert Hoover was president shantytowns were called Hoovervilles. It was an insult to the president.

Residents of many large cities could get meals at soup kitchens set up in church halls or public buildings. The meal usually consisted of a bowl of soup and a chunk of bread. Meals were usually free. Some soup kitchens were provided by

USING SCIENCE TO MEASURE OPINIONS

"I LOVE THE COWS AND CHICKENS, but I love them on the table," replied an unemployed man from Brooklyn, New York, when asked by a pollster if he would be willing to move to a farm rather than stay on relief in the city.

The interviewer worked for the American Institute of Public Opinion, a new organization under the direction of George Gallup. In 1935 the company began surveying Americans about major issues of the day. Mr. Gallup believed the average citizen was intelligent and capable of forming and expressing strong opinions that the nation's leaders should pay attention to.

Each week the Institute mailed ballots to about 200,000 people. Face-to-face interviews were also conducted. Using scientific methods to choose its respondents, the Institute ended up with a very realistic picture of the nation's feelings about important problems. Residents from every state were included. Rural as well as city dwellers were contacted. People from various income levels—including those on relief—were asked to give opinions. The results were tabulated and published in newspapers.

A great deal was learned about Americans:

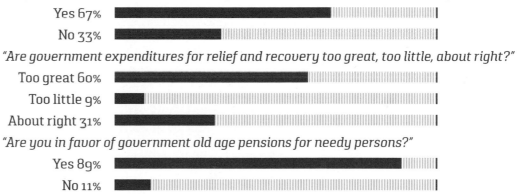

"Do you think this state should pass legislation making sit-down strikes illegal?"
Yes 67%
No 33%

"Are government expenditures for relief and recovery too great, too little, about right?"
Too great 60%
Too little 9%
About right 31%

"Are you in favor of government old age pensions for needy persons?"
Yes 89%
No 11%

Regarding the question asked to people on relief about their willingness to leave the city for a life on the farm, most were agreeable to a move. But it was a close vote: yes, 52 percent; no, 48 percent. One respondent expressed this opinion: "We wouldn't know what to do."

CONDUCT A SAMPLE SURVEY

GEORGE GALLUP started collecting data with surveys during the Depression. Use scientific methods to conduct a survey in your family, community, or school. This activity uses a random sampling.

You'll Need
- **Paper and pen**
- **Calculator**

1. Decide what issue you want to learn about. (For example: school lunches.)

2. Select your population. (Sixth grade.)

3. Use a lottery system to identify a sampling (a few members of the class) of the larger population (the entire class):

a. Give each sixth-grader a unique number on a slip of paper. Students must remember their numbers.

b. Throw all the numbers in a bowl.

c. Use 50 percent of your class as a sample. Have one student draw out enough numbers to equal 50 percent of your class. For example, if there are 80 sixth-graders, the student would select 40 slips from the bowl.

4. Design questions around your chosen topic, for example the school lunch pro-gram. Include several questions in order to get good data.

Here are a few examples:
Question 1: How would you rate the school lunches overall? Excellent, good, average, poor
Question 2: How would you rate the variety offered? Excellent, good, average, poor
Question 3: How would you rate the beverage selection? Excellent, good, average, poor

5. Give the questions to the students whose numbers were drawn in the lottery. Have respondents write down personal data on their answer sheets so that you can analyze your responses by gender, homeroom, time they eat lunch, etc.

6. Tabulate and analyze the data. Use percents to report each answer. Analyze according to the personal data provided by the respondents.

7. What conclusions can you draw? Write a statement to summarize your data.

churches or charitable agencies. Others were provided by city governments. In Chicago the city offered a soup kitchen that served meals and a place to sleep. Anyone with a dime slept on beds; others slept on the floor. In 1931 New York City was serving 85,000 meals a day to homeless New Yorkers.

Long lines called breadlines formed outside the soup kitchens as mealtimes approached. And while the soup kitchens were lifesavers for desperate people, many were ashamed to be seen standing on the street waiting for free food.

People scoured dumps and garbage piles for items they needed. Fuel for heating was expensive, so families looked for free resources. In New York City where the Empire State Building was under construction, truckloads of unused wood scraps were deposited on a vacant lot—free for the taking by people who needed them for heat.

People looked for ways to get food that didn't require them to stand in breadlines. One creative idea was to use vacant lots to grow vegetables and fruit. In Gary, Indiana, there were an estimated 20,000 gardens around the city. In Seattle 450 acres of land were dedicated to community gardens. In Iowa vacant lots were donated for use by jobless men and women in the summer of 1932. Vegetable seeds and fruit plantings were furnished to the men who planted, weeded, and harvested throughout the summer and fall. At harvest time home economics teachers showed women how to preserve food.

Early in the 1930s city, county, or state governments were responsible for providing aid to unemployed and poor families. Churches and charitable agencies also helped. Employed people donated part of their wages to help the unemployed. But as more and more people needed relief from the hardships of the Great Depression, Americans expected the *federal* government to offer assistance. In time, it did.

As the years of the Great Depression dragged on, city governments ran out of money. Income from taxes was down. People couldn't pay property taxes. Businesses had less money, so they paid less tax money to the city. On top of less money coming into the city accounts, more was going out for relief. Cities—as well as people—were suffering.

"I was paid until June 1931. When we came back, the city had gone broke," Elsa Ponselle said in a 1986 interview. She was a principal in a Chicago school during the Great Depression.

Elsa was one of about 14,000 Chicago teachers who continued teaching despite the end to paychecks in the early 1930s. "We were not going to hurt the children. We went on teaching, whether we were being paid or not," she recalled.

When the city could find money, teachers were paid. But sometimes months went by without pay. By spring 1933 some Chicago teachers were becoming impatient with the uncertainty. About 700 marched to the mayor's office demanding pay. They carried banners, sang songs, and heckled two city representatives.

Finally, in August 1934 relief was in sight for Chicago's educators. Funds from the

RELIEF FOR HORSES

"FEED, WATER, AND CARE FOR ME…pet me sometimes…do not take away my best defense against flies by cutting off my tail."

Estelle "Stella" Ehrlich reminded New York City horse owners of those words from "The Horse's Prayer." Stella had formed the Horse Aid Society of New York as a refuge for horses. With more people using automobiles and trucks, horses were in less demand. But some street peddlers and other business owners continued to use horses in the 1930s. Stella visited stables around the city and found too many animals in pitiful condition.

"How can I feed my horse when I cannot feed my children?" a poor horse owner asked Stella.

Stella had an answer: "Breadlines for horses." The best grade oats, hay, and alfalfa comprised the main course. Apples and carrots for dessert.

Stella opened an animal hotel for horses and other animals on a 40-acre farm in Millwood, New York. In addition to horses, the refuge housed donkeys, cats, dogs, and a goat.

Although the animals were happy on the farm, some neighbors were not pleased. They complained that barking dogs kept them awake at night. Cats wandered off the farm and chased wildlife. Horses whinnied. Donkeys brayed too loudly. (No complaints were issued about the goat.)

The Westchester County grand jury held an investigation of the animal hotel. Stella's attorney defended the establishment. "It's the Salvation Army of the animal world." The grand jury agreed—the charges were dismissed.

DRAW A LETTER MURAL

MURALS BEGAN TO POP UP in public spaces all over when a government project called the Federal Art Project was started in 1935. Combine your math and artistic skills to design and produce your own mural.

Adult supervision required

You'll Need

- 1 sheet 8½ by 11-inch (216 by 279-millimeter) of printer paper
- Ruler
- Pencil
- Colored pencil
- Clear tape
- A large slab of concrete, like a driveway
- Large pieces of colored sidewalk chalk
- Large straightedge (yardstick)
- Sticky notes
- Camera

1. Draw the first letter of your family name on a sheet of printer paper. Using a ruler, draw grid lines ½ by ½ inch (12.5 by 12.5 millimeters) over the image.

2. Number each square that has a shape in it.

3. With a parent or guardian's permission, move to the driveway or other approved con-

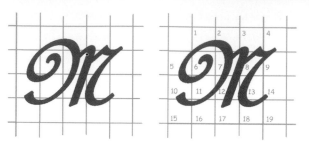

crete space where you will transfer your sketch to a full-scale surface. The surface must be very smooth. Your scale will be ½ inch = ½ foot. Look at your paper to see how many squares you need. Use a colored pencil (a contrasting color to the color of the surface) and a straightedge to draw a grid with the appropriate number of squares. For example, if your paper grid is 5 squares across and 4 squares down, the concrete grid will be 2½ feet by 2 feet. Each square will measure ½ foot by ½ foot.

4. Write a number on each sticky note. The numbers should correspond with the numbers in step 2. Place the sticky notes on the corresponding square drawn on the concrete. (You may need to use the clear tape if the adhesive on the sticky notes doesn't stick to the concrete.)

5. Using chalk, begin to transfer your drawing from the paper to the concrete. The paper grid gives you a point of reference for where everything goes. Look at each individual square on your paper to see where the lines fall in each square on the concrete grid. For example, look at square 1 on your paper, find square 1 on the concrete, draw the shape from the paper square 1 on the concrete square 1. Continue until you have your entire letter on the concrete.

6. Remove the paper number from the concrete as you complete that square. This helps you to keep track of where you are.

7. Take a picture because any precipitation will destroy your masterpiece.

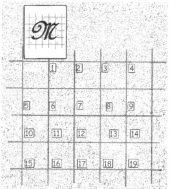
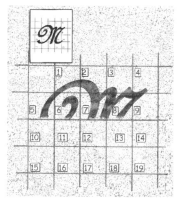

Reconstruction Finance Corporation that President Hoover had set up in 1932 and that had continued under President Roosevelt were used for schools. Over $22 million was paid to teachers who hadn't gotten paid in months.

WORKERS STRIKE

WHILE MANY Americans were looking for jobs in the 1930s, others who *had* jobs were refusing to work. Thousands of American workers decided to strike for higher wages and better working conditions during the Great Depression.

In 1934 Congress passed the National Industrial Recovery Act (NIRA). This new law guaranteed workers the right to form unions. Before the NIRA, workers who had tried to join unions were sometimes fired. With its passage, union organizers got busy forming new unions and increasing membership in existing ones.

Workers in many professions were eager to join. Plumbers, miners, newspaper writers, textile workers, truckers, farm workers, shipyard workers, and others joined the ranks of union labor. With unions behind them, workers were confident to strike for better wages and conditions. Major cities across the nation became sites of strikes during the Great Depression.

Businesses depended on ships to transport goods in the 1930s. Longshoremen, who loaded and unloaded huge cargo ships, had exhausting jobs. Many earned less than $10 per week. Some were forced to work 36 hours without sleep. It was difficult to get work—despite there being plenty of ships to load and unload. Each day men who wanted to work went to a hiring hall where shipping companies chose laborers for the day. But in San Francisco—and other cities—hiring foremen considered only the men who paid a bribe.

In the spring of 1934 members of the International Longshoremen's Association (ILA) in San Francisco went on strike—refusing to unload ships sitting in the port. Up and down the coast, from Seattle to San Diego, longshoremen joined the San Francisco men in sympathy. In addition, men in other shipping trades refused to work. Ships' crews walked off their jobs. Truckers who carried the ships' cargoes to warehouses or rail cars joined the strike. Construction of the Golden Gate Bridge was stopped because steel could not be delivered to the site.

Strikebreakers were hired to take over the jobs of the longshoremen. On July 5 the situation got out of control. Police and strikers clashed. Both sides used guns, rocks, and tear gas. At the end of the day over 60 people had been injured. Two men died. The day became known as "Bloody Thursday."

Later in the month a general strike was called. This meant workers all over the city decided to

This girl's parents were striking for better wages in California in 1938. Courtesy of the Library of Congress, Prints & Photographs Division, LC-DIG-fsa-8b32810

strike in support of the dock workers. Taxi drivers, barbers, auto mechanics, streetcar operators, and others struck. From July 16 to 19 the city of San Francisco was shut down. It was called the Great Strike.

In the end the ILA got most of the demands it had made. The long strike was considered a victory for the ILA and for labor unions in general. It proved that workers who joined unions could make changes for the better.

In December 1936 workers at the General Motors auto plant in Flint, Michigan, went on strike. They used a new strategy to get the attention of the bosses. They not only stopped working—they stayed at their posts inside the plant. This prevented the company from hiring strikebreakers. This new way of striking—called a sit-down strike—was effective. It took six weeks, but in the end the managers gave in to the workers, giving them higher wages.

Numerous strikes occurred throughout the 1930s in cities across the country. Truckers in Minneapolis, auto parts factory workers in Toledo, steelworkers in Chicago, and news writers in Seattle were among thousands of workers who valued their jobs during a time of economic depression. But they also believed they had a right to fair treatment by their employers.

Sometimes having a job during the Great Depression made little difference in the quality of life for families. If the pay was so low that families suffered from lack of food and fuel and if conditions were so dangerous that workers were injured, people were dissatisfied. They joined unions for protection. And they resorted to strikes when bosses ignored their demands. In some cases, having a dreadful job was worse than being unemployed.

Police were called in to handle striking dock workers in San Francisco in 1934.

A PERFECT PLACE to LIVE

STRIKES, OUT-OF-WORK people, a shortage of good housing. Add to that list of urban woes the problem of neglected and crumbling cities. The Great Depression had hurt the infrastructures of large cities. Streets, sidewalks, bridges, sewage and water plants, playgrounds, libraries, and schools were becoming run down. These structures were usually maintained with tax dollars. But the terrible economic situation meant there was little money for these projects. By the late 1930s some of America's cities were beginning to look very shabby.

As government leaders searched for solutions to the nation's problems, the idea of building model cities began to sound like a good idea. President Franklin Roosevelt chose Rexford Tugwell to develop the dream through an agency called the Resettlement Administration.

Greenbelt, Maryland, was one of three modern urban spaces built with federal funds as part of President Roosevelt's New Deal. The Emergency Relief Appropriation Act of 1935 provided funds for public works projects. Some of the money was used to construct public housing for needy Americans. Greenbelt and other cities were a result.

The cities of Greenbelt near Washington, DC, Greendale near Milwaukee, Wisconsin, and Greenhills near Cincinnati, Ohio, were

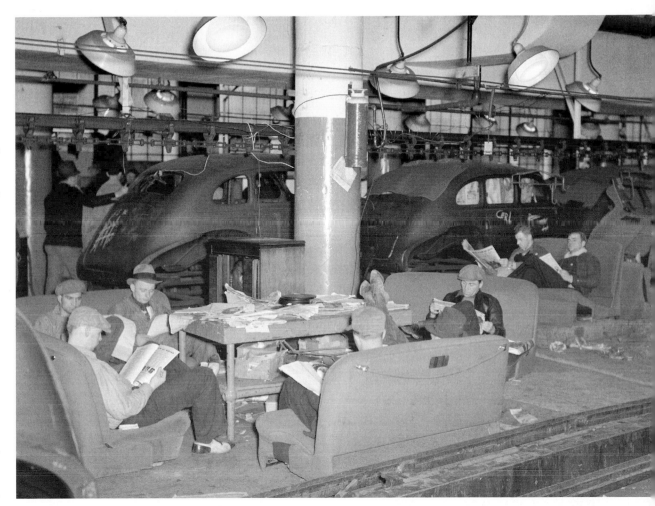

Strikers in a Michigan auto plant used sit-down strikes.
Courtesy of the Library of Congress, Prints & Photographs Division. LC-DIG-fsa-8c28669

built using government funds. They were unique because they were complete towns built where none had existed before. They were not only public *housing*; the projects also included schools, businesses, and recreation centers—entire communities subsidized by the government. Although residents paid rent for their houses, the government owned them and covered some of the costs of living there.

It was a massive undertaking. Work began in late 1935. Land was cleared in preparation for construction of roads and rail lines. Water and sewer facilities were built. Finally the workers constructed different-sized houses—one to four bedrooms with one bathroom.

By October 1937 residents were moving into Greenbelt. In the spring of 1938 Greenhills and Greendale were ready for occupancy.

People had to apply to live in the towns. Only families with incomes between $1,000 and $2,400 were considered. The government allowed only one family member to work outside the home. One-bedroom houses rented for $19 per month, four bedrooms for $32.50.

Many Americans resented the amount of money the government spent on the new towns. They were called "Tugwell Towns" by some critics as an insult to Rexford Tugwell. Many believed the towns were bad investments for the government.

"Never in the history of this country has there been such a waste of public money," a senator declared. Other critics were opposed to the federal government being in the "low cost housing business."

Despite the critics, families were eager to live in the new urban environments. Enthusiastic residents moved into their beautiful new homes.

Some homeowners rode the train into Washington to their jobs. Others worked at businesses in the community.

LeGrand Benefiel and June Zoellner were fifth-graders at Greenbelt school in 1939. If they were aware of the controversy surrounding their community, they didn't let it interfere with their enthusiasm for their schoolwork. The school curriculum was carefully chosen to expose students to environmental issues, or "conservation." A news reporter who visited the school said the kids "talk conservation morning, noon, and night."

LeGrand and June's class had built a relief map of North America that covered the floor of their classroom. They and their classmates used 25 pounds of flour and 18 pounds of salt mixed with water to form mountains and other features as they learned about geography and science.

WORLD FAIRS PERK UP CITY LIFE

"A wonderland where everything you have ever dreamed about will come true."

THAT'S WHAT the planners of the Chicago World's Fair of 1933—called the Century of Progress—promised kids who visited the Enchanted Island inside the fairgrounds.

Greenbelt schoolchildren.

CONSTRUCT A RELIEF MAP

CONSERVATION of land and natural resources became an important issue after much of the nation's topsoil was destroyed by unwise farming practices. Students in one of the Tugwell Towns learned about land and natural resources by constructing a giant relief map in their school.

You'll Need

- Homemade dough (see recipe below)
- Foam board
- Butcher paper
- Markers
- Computer with internet access
- Flag-shaped labels
- Toothpicks
- Various colors of watercolor paint and a brush

DOUGH RECIPE

Mix together:
- 4 cups flour
- 2 cups salt
- 2 tablespoons cream of tartar

Add:
- 2 cups water

Mix with your hands.

Draw the outline shape of a geographic location (a state or country, for example) on a piece of foam board lined with butcher paper.

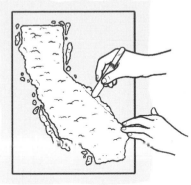

Spread dough over and within the lines of the geographic shape. Make the surface as flat and smooth as possible. A rolling pin helps, but stay within the lines of the shape. If you go outside of the lines, use a table knife to trim the edges. Save some dough to form geographic features.

Look at an online relief map of the geographic region you are replicating. What land forms do you see? Are there lakes, rivers, mountains, or hills?

Form the land features in the dough. Cut rivers into the surface. Scoop out lakes. Identify major cities and other landmarks with toothpicks and flag-shaped labels.

When the dough has dried and hardened (after about 24 hours), use watercolor paint to add appropriate color to the relief map—blue for water, green for vegetation, etc. Don't forget to color or add designs to the butcher paper "trim" around the outline for added interest. You could include objects that are representative of the state or country. These could be painted, or make them in relief with scraps of the dough when you are forming the original features.

It turned out to be true for Darwin Reed, a seven-year-old from Illinois. As he walked through the entrance of the Enchanted Island on August 22, Darwin was greeted by a seven-foot giant and a gaggle of clowns. Hundreds of kids cheered and shouted as it was announced, "You are the one millionth youngster to visit this island." Darwin was stunned but quickly recovered when he was rewarded with a shiny new wagon and bicycle.

The Enchanted Island was one of the many attractions where Depression-weary Americans could forget their troubles for a few hours. Adults marveled at the House of Tomorrow where they learned about automatic dishwashers and air-conditioning. Visitors experienced the "supreme thrill of the fair" riding rocket cars suspended 200 feet above the fairgrounds.

Darwin Reed and the other children who entered the Enchanted Island climbed the Magic Mountain to the Fairy Castle at the top where they propelled down a "mysterious spiral slide." A miniature train carried the kids around the island. Some stopped at the Monkey Island where "squeaking, chattering, and mimicking" monkeys greeted them.

"Scandalous John" the bull visits Washington, DC, on his way to the New York World's Fair.
Courtesy of the Library of Congress, Prints & Photographs Division, LC-DIG-hec-26440

World fairs had been popular attractions during the late 1800s and early 1900s. Exhibitions and performances demonstrated the progress made by countries in the areas of science, technology, and the arts. The fairs were opportunities for cities to showcase their ability to produce spectacular events. The stubborn economic problems of the Great Depression made some cities fearful to sponsor these extravaganzas. With so many unemployed and so many businesses failing, maybe no one would come to the fairs. It was a huge risk.

Several cities saw a fair as an opportunity to promote spending by consumers—always helpful to the economy. San Diego, San Francisco, Cleveland, Dallas, and New York City all hosted world fairs during the 1930s. The 1939 New York fair, called the World of Tomorrow, inspired hope for the future—a future without soup kitchens, breadlines, and shantytowns. The fairs proved that even in times of great hardship people were excited to celebrate their progress and look to a brighter future.

A North Dakota field, ruined by grasshoppers.

Courtesy of the Library of Congress, Prints & Photographs Division, LC-DIG-fsa-8b28099

DROUGHTS, DUST STORMS, *and* PEST PLAGUES— RURAL LIFE

Americans could blame a failing economy on the folly of fellow humans— lack of leadership by government officials, excessive greed of investors, and foreclosures by heartless bankers. The terrible natural disasters that swept the country during the 1930s were products of Mother Nature. Foolish humans and Mother Nature seemed to throw all they had at Americans during the 1930s.

WINGED INVADERS

"They came mysteriously, and they left, with havoc behind them..."

AN INVASION was sweeping the country. From California, Montana, and Colorado to South Dakota, Nebraska, and Iowa, swarms of grasshoppers devoured wheat, corn, and potato fields as well as lawns and trees.

A mass of insects 50 feet wide and half a mile long inched its way across 400 acres near the shores of Lake Tahoe, California. In Nebraska they made railroad tracks so slippery that trains had trouble moving over the rails. In South Dakota one farmer turned his turkey flock into the infested fields to eat the grasshoppers, but they returned featherless. In Kansas women complained of the pests lurking behind pictures on the walls, beneath rugs, and in parlor sofas. A farmer's perspiration-soaked gloves were devoured by the salt-craving creatures.

Grasshoppers were just one reminder for farmers that they were at the mercy of Mother Nature. During the 1930s one natural disaster after another struck, leaving farmers with damaged soil and ruined crops. When it happened year after year, it was too much for some who made their living from the land.

MASSIVE FLOODS LEAVE PEOPLE and ANIMALS HOMELESS

WHEN THE Republican River overflowed its banks in May 1935, people climbed trees to escape the raging floodwaters. When they got to the top, they found they weren't alone. Snakes had made temporary homes in the treetops. It was the only safe place.

Communities along the flood path in Colorado, Kansas, and Nebraska were devastated. As the waters subsided, people started the recovery process. Farmers found the bodies of their horses, cattle, and hogs packed into sandbars and drifting down the river. Driftwood and trash covered their farmland. A fine silt lay over their fields.

Over 20,000 farm animals died across the three states. Over 275,000 acres of farmland were damaged. The human toil was overwhelming as survivors searched for lost loved ones. Some were never recovered; 110 people died.

Three floods in the 1930s brought havoc to people living in Texas's Colorado River basin. Central Texas had barely recovered from one when another hit. Almost 30 inches of rain fell in May and June 1935. A year later two storms dropped 51 inches of rain. Farmhouses and livestock were destroyed along the Concho River, a tributary of the Colorado River. In 1938, over a 10-day period, 25 inches rained over the towns and farms of the area. More than 4,000 farm and town families were left homeless.

"The situation is dangerous and people are greatly alarmed. We could hear the roar as the levee gave way and the water came plunging over," Marion Groh wrote in her diary of her experiences during the Ohio River Great Flood of January 1937. She lived in New Albany, Indiana, where floodwaters covered the streets and surrounded her family's home.

Indiana was one of several states along the Ohio and Mississippi Rivers that suffered from floodwaters in the winter of 1937. Excessive rains in a matter of a few days caused the rivers and their tributaries to overflow. Up and down the two river valleys, people in 11 states fled their homes. Some took shelter in camps set up by the government.

In Arkansas over a million acres of farmland were affected. Thousands of farmers and share-croppers were left homeless. Tent cities were constructed to offer refuge. Farm families were offered pens for the animals they saved from the floodwaters. It was estimated that 20,000 mules, cows, dogs, cats, and chickens were rescued. Despite their efforts, over 34,000 animals were destroyed.

In Cairo, Illinois, the Army Corps of Engineers decided to dynamite a levee upstream

THE GRASSHOPPER EXTERMINATOR

WITH REPORTS OF MOUNDS OF GRASS-HOPPERS making rails so slick that passenger trains had to travel at a snail's pace, farmers' gloves being chewed to shreds, and wooden pitchfork handles gnawed to splinters, everyone was looking for the solution to this maddening plague.

Farmers and entomologists were willing to try anything. In some midwestern states they mixed a concoction of bran moistened with molasses—a favorite of the pests—to attract them. However, the tasty treat was laced with poison to make the feast a last meal for the devouring insects. In Colorado they sprayed as many as they could catch with pink, green, or blue paint so scientists could trace their flights—hoping to learn more about the pesky little creatures' habits.

Despite all the efforts of scientists and farmers, nothing seemed to work. Creative

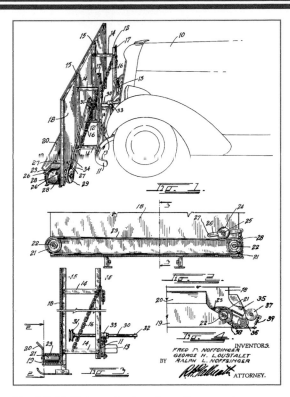

Fred P. Noffsinger's drawing of a grasshopper exterminator. Courtesy Google Patents

inventors designed contraptions that promised to rid the land of the destructive menace. Fred P. Noffsinger developed a "grasshopper exterminator" and filed a patent for his invention. His portable device could be attached to any vehicle, which was driven across a grasshopper-infested area. As the vehicle moved forward, the insects jumped against the vertical metal back plate and fell into a moving belt. They were carried beneath a roller where they were crushed. The bodies were spewed out onto the field or roadway as a powdery green dust.

Family living in a boxcar after losing their home to a flood. Courtesy of the Library of Congress, Prints & Photographs Division. LC-DIG-fsa-8b30115

from the town. It was controversial because by doing so the velocity and depth of the gushing waters that hit Cairo would be reduced, but it meant volumes of water would spread over acres of farmland. Still, many believed the action was fair because it saved lives.

THE DUST BOWL

"Endless miles of usually rich, fertile farm- lands lie scorched, blighted, literally baked. All vegetation is scarred, stunted, ruined. Cattle are starving, dying of thirst."

NATURE HAD thrown its mighty force at farm- ers during the 1930s with armies of insects and colossal floods. But there was even more to come. It came in the form of endless days of scorching heat and rainless skies. Howling winds swept up rich topsoil and replaced it with dunes of dust.

For years farmers had plowed up the prairie grasses and cut down trees to plant season after season of crops. The soil was exhausted and no longer had the necessary nutrients to feed plants. It hadn't had a rest in a long time. Livestock had been allowed to eat all the vegetation, leaving bare land.

Drought conditions existed in many states early in the 1930s. Day after day of 100°F temperatures with little rain in sight took a toll on farmland and crops. By the mid-1930s the drought was coupled

with high winds. With nothing covering the land, the winds scooped up the topsoil and left nothing but sandy soil behind.

The winds swept across Kansas, Oklahoma, Texas, Arkansas, Colorado, and New Mexico and deposited dust in banks along fencerows and against buildings. People called the storms "black blizzards." Housewives hung wet sheets over doors and windows to keep the dust from creeping into their houses. People used masks to keep the dust out of their mouths and lungs. Schools and businesses closed. Low visibility caused delays in travel. The area became known as the Dust Bowl. And the years of the Dust Bowl were called the "dirty thirties."

"The dust piled to the top of a three-and-a- half-foot fence and started to bank around the house," a Kansas farmer said.

The fine dust came into the houses through the tiniest cracks and crevices. Floors were gritty. People became sick from the dirt in their nos- trils and lungs. They coughed up dirt. Animals died from the constant dust in their lungs and stomachs.

"The big field looks like an ocean of dirt," the weary Kansas farmer observed. "We're mighty tired of digging out dirt, but we know this won't last. I've got faith in this land."

In April 1935, 10-year-old Ben Moril Cloud learned how dangerous dust storms could be. As the school bus dropped Ben off near his farmhouse near Winona, Kansas, one afternoon he noticed the wind picking up. He had no idea what lay ahead of him.

"I saw little whirls here and there, but then I noticed a great storm was coming and I started to run for home," Ben explained later. "Then I saw the storm would cut me off, so I started for a neighbor's house."

Before Ben could reach the neighbors it was "pitch black," he said. He lost sight of the house and everything else. All he could see was swirling dust. He wandered for a while as he tried to get

SIMULATE A WINDSTORM

FARMERS FAILED TO USE wise conservation practices in the 1920s and '30s. This led to the Dust Bowl, which picked up acres of loose topsoil, leaving dust and useless soil behind. If farmers had left the stubble of their crops in the ground instead of plowing it up, the roots would have held the soil in place.

By using a simple conservation technique, you will demonstrate the value of plants in preventing wind erosion.

You'll Need
- Two flat, shallow, waterproof containers (about 11 by 13 inches [279 by 330 millimeters] and 3 to 4 inches [76 to 102 millimeters] high)
- 1 small bag of potting soil
- Marker
- 1 or 2 packets of seeds—flower, grass, or vegetable
- Hair dryer
- Old newspapers

1. Pour the potting soil into the containers, spreading it evenly between the two. It should be 2 to 3 inches (51 to 76 millimeters) deep. (Keep a little aside to use in step 2.)

2. Label one container "Seeds." Sprinkle the seeds evenly over the soil. Cover them with a light layer of soil. Water gently so as not to disturb the seeds. Set both containers aside. The one with seeds should be placed in a warm, sunny location.

3. Do not water the container that holds soil only. Gently sprinkle the seed container with water every other day. Soon tiny shoots will appear. When they are 1 to 2 inches (25 to 51 millimeters) tall, it's time to simulate a windstorm.

4. Set the two containers side by side on old newspapers (for easy cleanup). Use a hair dryer at its lowest speed and blow over the two containers. What happens to the soil in each? Next, increase the speed. Now what happens?

Your simulation should show that the moist, seeded soil stays in place much better than the dry, unseeded soil. Do research to learn other methods to keep soil from eroding. Possible sources for information are the Environmental Protection Agency, Bureau of Land Management, US Department of Agriculture, and your state department of natural resources.

his bearings. But soon he knew it was hopeless, and the wind didn't show any sign of easing.

Ben's dad had warned him about dust storms. He had told him not to run, but to stay in place until the winds died down. Ben knew it could be hours before that happened. So he gathered as much soap weed as he could to make a bed. He lay on the pile to keep it from blowing away. Ben woke once during the night, but the wind was still howling, and it had begun to snow. When he awoke again it was daylight and the wind, dust, and snow had stopped. He looked around and discovered he was only a short distance from a friend's house.

MOVING WEST

"My farm moved out from under me . . . everything dried up and blowed away. The papers said they needed a lot of farmers out here."

J. B. THOMPSON explained how he ended up living in a tent in California with his wife and children. The Thompsons had been farmers in Oklahoma in the early 1930s, but by 1938 they found themselves picking cotton for a huge farming operation on the West Coast.

They were among the thousands of farmers who had tried to make a living farming despite the pests, floods, droughts, and dust storms that had destroyed the once-rich topsoil in the Great Plains. Giving up after years of hardships, they packed up the few possessions they had and fled the Dust Bowl region, searching for work as migrant laborers on farms along the West Coast, where they heard workers were needed in the fields. They moved with the seasons, planting in the spring, harvesting in the fall. They plowed, planted, pruned, picked, sorted, packed, and canned the fruits and vegetables enjoyed by millions across the country. Many, like the Thompsons, picked cotton.

"Cotton pickin' season's 'bout over an' now we got to leave an' we don't know where to go," J. B. said.

Although the Thompsons didn't know where they would go next, they had a good idea of what their living conditions would be. The life of migrant workers was a harsh one.

The company that owned the acres of farmland provided the workers with rickety shacks or flimsy tents on wooden platforms. Each structure was nine feet by nine feet. When it rained the floorboards became soaked. The workers used fire hydrants set up in the roadways between the shacks for drinking, washing, and cooking. People stood in line to use the outhouses.

If these displaced farmers from the central United States thought their new lives as farm workers in the West would be easier and more

Baby in migrant camp, 1939.

profitable than farming, they were to be disappointed. But as J. B. Thompson said, "We had to do somethin'. Had to eat, you know."

Farmers in the 1930s faced a variety of natural disasters. They knew they were limited in their ability to control nature. But if dealing with nature was frustrating to America's farmers, handling the economic trials was even more confounding. It seemed no one could answer the question, "When will the economy turn around?"

FARMERS REVOLT

MRS. E. P. BAACK owned the Craig Mercantile Store in Craig, Iowa, in 1932. Most mornings she traveled in her truck to nearby Sioux City to get merchandise for the store. One morning in September on her way into the city, she saw groups of men standing along the road. As she approached they began moving into the roadway—waving their arms and shouting at her as she slowed down to avoid hitting anyone.

"We'll get you!" they shouted as she slowly moved forward.

Mrs. Baack made it to Sioux City and picked up her supplies. On her return trip she again saw the men. Now there was a line of trucks behind and in front of Mrs. Baack. The men began throwing spiked logs, pieces of iron, poles, and rocks into the roadway and at the trucks. Windshields were smashed. Several truckers ended up with scratches and bruises. One sustained a broken shoulder. Mrs. Baack was not injured.

The men who caused all the chaos were farmers who belonged to the Farmers Holiday Association. Members decided to call a "holiday" of farm goods. They refused to do business until they got higher prices for their produce—corn, wheat, livestock, and milk. Their slogan was "Stay at Home—Buy Nothing—Sell Nothing." They hoped Americans would complain when they weren't able to buy the food they wanted. And that would lead to better prices for farmers.

Sometimes striking farmers were determined to keep products from the markets. They stopped trucks hauling milk and dumped it on the roads. They stopped a truck hauling butter and smeared the yellow mess all over the pavement. The slippery slime caused cars to slip into the ditches.

Before the months-long holiday was over in Iowa, plenty of damage had been done, and farmers hadn't gotten higher prices. People were arrested. Men had been injured, and one man was killed. Farmers in other states followed the example of Iowa farmers and declared holidays too. Some ended in violence.

The Farmers Holiday Association got a lot of attention. But only a very small number of farmers belonged to the group, and not all resorted to violence. However, all farmers across the country were hurting during the 1920s and '30s, and most were frustrated and worried.

Farmers were right to be worried. They were making far less money on their products than in the years of the Great War. Wheat had fetched $3 per bushel in the war years and only 30 cents per bushel in 1932. They had gotten as much as $1.23 per bushel for corn; in 1932 farmers made only 15 cents per bushel. Five cents per pound for cotton was much less than in previous years. It bothered farmers to see a quart of milk selling for 8 cents in the stores when they were getting only 2 cents as their share of the profits. These low prices made it difficult for farmers to purchase the things their families needed. It was estimated that a whole wagon full of oats wouldn't buy a pair of shoes that cost $4 in 1932. Corn prices were so low that some families burned it for fuel because it was cheaper than coal.

FARM HEROINES of the NATION

IN SEPTEMBER 1935 Eleanor Waters visited a bank in Montgomery County, Maryland, hoping to borrow $50,000. She represented a group called the Montgomery Farm Women's Cooperative Market. The women wanted to buy the building that housed their farmers' market.

A couple of years before, 19 farm women had formed the cooperative to sell their farm products to the residents of Washington, DC, and the suburbs surrounding the city. They had been very successful selling baked goods, canned fruits and vegetables, and poultry and dairy products.

Eleanor said the bank president thought she was crazy. He was reluctant to make the loan to

MAKE HOMEMADE WHIPPED CREAM

WOMEN WHIPPED CREAM to add to desserts. This luscious topping was especially rich when made with thick cream fresh off the farm.

Today ready-made whipped topping is available in the freezer section of the grocery store. But you can make homemade topping just as cooks during the Great Depression did.

Adult supervision required

You'll Need

Utensils
- Steel bowl
- Electric mixer
- Spatula

Ingredients
- 1 cup heavy cream
- 2 tablespoons powdered sugar
- ½ teaspoon vanilla extract

Optional flavorings:
- 2 tablespoons unsweetened cocoa powder plus 1 tablespoon additional sugar; or
- ½ teaspoon finely shredded orange, lemon, or lime peel; or
- ¼ teaspoon cinnamon; or
- 4 cups fresh sliced strawberries

About an hour before beginning the process, place the bowl and the electric mixer's beaters in the freezer.

Remove the cold utensils and attach the chilled beaters to the mixer.

Place the cream, powdered sugar, and vanilla in the bowl. Beat on medium speed until soft peaks form.

Add optional flavoring if desired.

Serve on top of fresh sliced strawberries.

Serves 4

In the 1930s cooks would have used an egg beater similar to this.

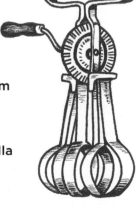

a group of farm women who he thought would have a difficult time repaying the money. But he was surprised when he accepted their invitation to visit the site on a market day. When he saw the brisk business the women were stirring up in the deepest days of the Great Depression, he agreed to the loan on the spot! (The market is still going strong in the same location today.)

Although the Montgomery County banker was surprised at the ambitious farm women in his county, others around the country were not surprised by the grit of farm women. After all, many of them were descendants of pioneer women.

The farm women of America showed just how tough they could be during the Great Depression. In 1935, 90 percent of the nation's farmers lived without electricity. That meant farm women cooked, canned, and cleaned without refrigerators or appliances. They used kerosene lamps and wood cook stoves. Food was cooled in iceboxes kept cold with huge blocks of ice. Women did laundry without running water.

Farm women became very resourceful when making clothes for their families. Dad's clothes were cut down for small sons. Underwear for the entire family was made from the fabric sacks that flour and seed came in from the store. Holes in clothes were patched. Tears were mended. The good parts of ragged towels were cut down for washcloths. Scraps of fabric left over from sew-ing projects were made into quilts. Nothing was thrown away.

Farm families had plenty of land to have big gardens. Women oversaw the tilling, planting, weeding, and harvesting of the produce. It was wonderful to have all those luscious fresh fruits and vegetables in the summer, but they also had to last through the winter. It was up to the women to preserve them. They canned and pick-led food—both long, tiring processes.

When the women weren't working in the house, they worked in the barns and fields, all the while giving birth to and raising multiple children. It wasn't unusual for farm families to have 10 or more children.

The University of Vermont decided to find out how many miles a woman covered in an average day on the farm. Thirty women were given pedometers to wear for a week. It was found that they covered from three to nine miles each day. It was estimated that farm women spent an average of 63 hours a week just doing housework. That didn't include the hours spent outside the house.

Because farmers were getting such terrible prices for their livestock and crops, the women came up with creative ways for making money. They sold their canned goods, jams, baked goods, and small animals such as cats and birds. They made braided rugs and sold them, along with other crafts. Sometimes farm women earned

DESIGN A PAPER QUILT BLOCK

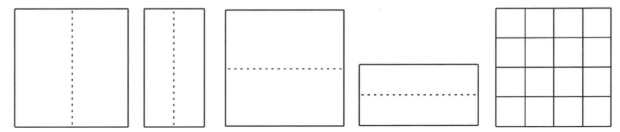

BLANKETS PURCHASED AT A STORE were too expensive for many large farm families. Women recycled and pieced together fabric scraps to form a blanket or quilt that cost little more than many hours of stitching. A real fabric quilt would consist of many small blocks sewn together. These beautiful quilts kept families warm and were often lovely works of art. You will design one paper quilt block. Although yours won't be useful as a blanket, it will be a pleasing piece of art.

You'll Need
- 1 sheet white paper, 8 by 8 inches (203 by 203 millimeters)
- Pencil
- Straightedge or ruler
- 1 sheet white posterboard
- Markers

1. Quilts sometimes have a theme that tells a story through shapes and colors. Decide on a theme for your block. The colors and shapes could reflect your school or favorite sports team.

2. Make a practice template where you will lay out your design before putting it on the posterboard.

a. Take a square of white paper and fold it in half vertically. Now you have a rectangle.

b. Fold the rectangle in half again vertically.

3. Open the paper. Repeat the two steps, folding the other way, horizontally.

4. Open the paper. You now have a paper with 16 squares (the fold lines are your grid).

5. Draw your design on the practice grid. Use a pencil and straightedge to create rectangles, squares, and triangles within each square in your design. Choose three different colors for your design. Assign each color a number. For example: color 1 = red; color 2 = white; color 3 = blue. Use symmetry to guide your choices of shapes and colors.

6. Use your template as a model to recreate your design on a sturdier surface such as white posterboard.

7. Cut the board to 8 by 8 inches (203 by 203 millimeters).

8. Using a sharp pencil and a ruler, lightly draw the grid lines to form 16 2-inch squares. Refer to your template to add the lines for the rectangles, squares, and triangles of your design.

9. Use colored markers to fill in the colors according to your design template.

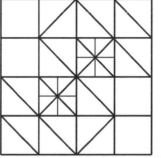
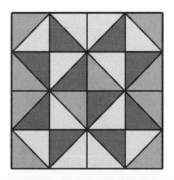

RE-CREATE DEPRESSION GLASS

IN THIS ACTIVITY you will do what many Americans did every day during the Great Depression—reuse and recycle. You will reuse a glass container and make it look like Depression glass. Do some research to learn about this attractive kind of dishware. It often came in pastel yellow, green, or pink and looked very delicate and almost lacy. Find pictures online or visit an antique store. Add a bouquet of handcrafted paper flowers to your container for a wonderful handmade Mother's Day gift or just to enjoy yourself.

Adult supervision required

You'll Need

For the container:

* 1 cup vinegar
* ¼ cup water
* 1 clear glass jar or bottle from the recycling bin
* Acrylic craft paint
* 3 foam brushes
* White craft glue

For the paper flowers:

* 8 pieces tissue paper of any size
* Ruler
* 1 pipe cleaner

1. Mix the vinegar and water together and wash the jar inside and out with the mixture.

2. Dry the jar. Apply a thin, even coat of the craft paint. Let the paint dry for 24 hours.

3. Using a foam brush, spread white glue over the paint on the jar. Slather it on in all directions and vary the thickness.

4. Let the glue dry a little. (It should still be tacky to the touch.)

5. Apply a second layer of paint. You will see a crackle effect begin to form. While it's not Depression glassware, your recycled vase is pretty and avoided the landfill.

TO MAKE A PAPER BOUQUET:

1. Place eight pieces of tissue paper of any color flat on top of each other.

2. Start at one end and fold the paper into a 1-inch fold across the width of the paper. Flip the paper and make a back fold—as though you were making a paper fan. Continue folding and flipping until you reach the end of the paper.

3. Grasp the middle of the "fan."

4. Twist a pipe cleaner around the middle.

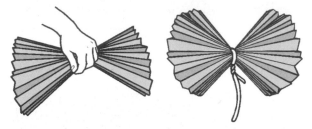

5. Cut or tear the ends of the fan through all of the thicknesses. Cut a V, or tear a jagged edge.

6. Starting with the first piece of paper closest to the middle, pull each piece up toward the middle. Do this until all of the papers are pulled to the center.

7. Repeat on the other side of the pipe cleaner until the flower is complete.

money by babysitting or taking in sewing and mending from others.

Many farm women raised chickens and other poultry. They sold the eggs and their butchered chickens. The money they made was called their "egg money." They also milked cows and sold milk, butter, and cheese. Of course, that entailed bottling the milk, churning the butter, and processing the cheese.

It was a common practice for farm women to sell or barter their produce with the local grocer. They took the items to the nearest town, and the grocer took their items in exchange for groceries like sugar or flour.

It was difficult to estimate just how much money women generated for their work on the farms across the country. But all their baking, canning, and cooking meant their families didn't have to purchase as much food. And by sewing their families' clothes, women spent fewer of their precious dollars at the stores buying expensive pants, shirts, and dresses.

In Georgia experts estimated that 14,000 women in 28 counties marketed more than $1 million in farm products in 1932. That included $250,000 of canned fruits and $300,000 of green produce, poultry, and dairy products. Girls in 4-H clubs had packaged over 4,500 containers of food. In 1933 North Carolina farm women's farmers' markets brought in $300,000.

These reports of the contributions of farm women to the economy prompted a *Washington Post* reporter to label them "the farm heroines of the nation."

TENANT FARMERS

MALE OR female. Black or white. Farming in the 1930s was a harsh way to make a living. The harsh conditions forced some farmers to become tenants. This meant they did not own the land they farmed; rather, they rented the land from the owner. Some tenants were sharecroppers. They provided the labor for a landowner, who supplied the seed, tools, and machinery. The sharecropper and the landowner split the earnings after the harvest. The sharecropping system varied from farm to farm, but life as a sharecropper was seldom a good situation.

In 1935 there were 6.8 million farmers in the United States, and 2.8 million were tenants. Many tenant farmers and sharecroppers were African Americans. In 1930, of the 835,000 black men who were engaged in farming in the South, only 13 percent were landowners. The rest were tenants.

The tenants and sharecroppers lived in houses furnished by the landowner. There were usually three rooms with windows but no screens, so insects moved in and out freely. Their bathrooms

were outdoor privies. The drinking water often came from contaminated wells.

Some landowners cheated their sharecroppers when it came time to settle up. The landowners kept the books, so the laborers had to rely on the honesty of the landowners. Many sharecroppers were illiterate, so they couldn't scrutinize the records. Some landowners paid their tenants in scrip—money that could be spent only at the local store, which was owned by the landowner. For many sharecroppers and tenants, there was no way out.

In the late 1930s Lula Wright, a black tenant farmer in Alabama, talked about her life. "I went to school 'til I was in fifth grade. We always had to stop and to go work in the fields in March."

Lula had spent her entire life doing farmwork. As an adult she was a tenant on an old plantation owned by a family named Green. They grew cotton. She lived in a one-room house with a fireplace to heat the room. All the cooking was done over the open fire. Lula stretched old coats over the window openings to keep the cold wind out. There was no glass in the openings—just boards.

"This old shack—so open. We beg Mrs. Green to fix it, but she won't do it. She won't give us a nail to fix anything."

Lula explained how the system worked on the Green farm, where the landowners got two-thirds of the crop Lula harvested. "I just made three bales of cotton last year. One bale goes for rent. One bale for fertilizer and to run the farm. One bale to get clothes and food." Lula had little left after paying off all her expenses.

The actions of humans and the forces of Mother Nature united to make life in rural areas difficult for many in the 1920s and '30s. Tenants and farm owners faced hard times, and that affected other people living in rural areas. Shopkeepers and business owners—and those who worked for them—suffered too. Some families chose to give up and move to cities where they hoped to find better conditions. Others stayed on the farms and small towns hoping to outlast the harsh economic times and survive the daunting forces of nature.

A "jungle," or homeless camp, near St. Louis, Missouri.

Courtesy of the Library of Congress, Prints & Photographs Division, LC-DIG-fsa-8b27090

GROWING UP *in* TOUGH TIMES

Patience Abbe was 12 years old in 1936. Her friends were movie stars. She had traveled all over Europe. And, along with her two brothers, she had written a bestselling book titled *Around the World*. It was the midst of the Great Depression, but Patience had an enviable lifestyle. Her dad was a noted photographer who captured images of stars and political figures around the globe. He took his family along on his trips; that's how Patience happened to write her very funny but insightful book about life on the road.

At about the time Patience was roaming the world with her family, a 15-year-old boy who called himself "Happy Joe" was traveling too. But he was riding the rails across America looking for work. Originally from New York, Happy Joe hopped freight trains to carry him from town to town.

"Dad lost his job. Nobody could get work. Then I lost my job. When I read they were hiring in Detroit I went there. I stayed there for a while. Then I just traveled," Happy Joe explained.

Dressed in a man's coat that he pinned up to keep it from dragging on the ground, Happy Joe slept and ate in outdoor camps near the tracks, where he could easily hop the next train. There were other boys and girls at the camps, or "jungles," as they were called. These kids were in similar situations. Most had left their homes because their families were in stressful situations.

"Texas" came from a family with seven kids and two parents who wanted to work but lost their jobs. When Texas lost his job as a shoe shine boy, he took off so there would be one less mouth to feed. "Since then, I just been traveling," he said.

A young girl called "Spit" claimed she left home because "Mother never liked me." Vera from New Jersey was tired of her mother's flightiness when it came to marriage—she had been married 11 times, and Vera just couldn't tolerate another stepfather. Jennie from Pennsylvania left home when her mother died. "Dad tried to keep a home for the four of us kids. I was willing to work, but nobody hired me. I just sort of scrammed."

Life for most kids during the Great Depression fell somewhere between the experiences of the Abbe family and those of the homeless kids who rode the rails.

SCHOOL DAYS

"A country school offers a wholesome environment. . . . Our schools are situated in the midst of the Del Monte Pine Forest on the Monterey Peninsula. There are miles of trails through the woods and over sand dunes by the sea."

GRACE PARSONS DOUGLAS described the school she ran at Pebble Beach, California, in 1933. The Douglas School for Girls and its counterpart for boys offered swimming, golf, horseback riding, tennis, and archery in addition to academic courses. Although the Douglas schools were country schools, they were very different from the country schools found in most rural areas of America in the 1930s.

One-room country schools offered eight grades taught by one teacher. After the eighth grade, students might attend a high school in a nearby town or city. Often formal education ended after eighth grade. The school calendar revolved around the planting and harvesting of crops.

Rural schools were heated with wood or coal stoves. There was no electricity. Kerosene lamps provided light. Restrooms were outdoor privies. The water supply came from a pump located outside. All the kids drank out of the same ladle dipped into a bucket.

Most kids walked to school. Some rode horses or drove a wagon pulled by a horse. They brought lunches their mothers had packed. Recess was held outside. Playground equipment was sparse. Kids played games like tag or ran foot races.

A good LUNCH

ONE HOT DISH
meat   vegetables

SANDWICH

FRUIT

MILK

WPA SCHOOL LUNCH

Some schools offered hot lunches for the first time.

Courtesy of the Library of Congress, Prints & Photographs Division, LC-USZC2-5427

PLAY "ROUND BALL"

TIMES WERE TOUGH, so playtime was important to kids during the Great Depression. Expensive store-bought games were not part of life for most families or schools. They had to invent their own or rely on old standbys that kids had played for years. Round ball was a fun time and didn't require expensive equipment—just a couple of balls.

You'll Need
- 20–60 players
- 2 basketball-sized balls

All the players make a wide circle by holding hands. To make the circle bigger, all the players drop hands and move backward two big steps. Number off in twos: "One, two," "One, two" until all players have said a number. The first "number one" is captain of the Ones team. The first "number two" is captain for the Twos. It may help to have each team wear an identifying "uniform" such as hats or the same color T-shirts, because if the team is big it's difficult to remember who's on your team.

Each captain has a ball and begins the game by throwing it either left or right to the member of his or her team (ones to ones, twos to twos) who is closest to him or her in the circle. Team members continue to throw the ball around the circle in the same direction to the team member who is closest to him or her.

The team whose ball completes the circle five times first wins. Each time the captain receives the ball, he or she calls out a number corresponding to the number of times the ball has circulated—one for the first time, two for the second time, etc. Play should be rapid. If a player drops the ball it must go back to the first team member to start over, costing valuable time.

The game may be varied by requiring different methods of throwing and catching—for example, catching with the right or left hand only.

(Adapted from *Games for the Playground, Home, School, and Gymnasium* [1909] by Jessie Hubbell Bancroft.)

With only a single teacher to direct the learning of all the different grade levels, students had to work independently. Older kids helped the younger ones. The main subjects were reading, writing, and arithmetic.

Schools were segregated by race. African American students went to schools that were supposed to be "separate but equal." They were almost never equal. The buildings were run down. Supplies were second rate. Textbooks that were discarded by the white schools ended up at the black schools.

"[S]chool histories . . . we do know that they are unjust to the life of our people . . ." a Native American leader expressed his concern about the way in which his people were portrayed in history textbooks in the 1930s. America's schoolchildren learned a very lopsided version of the role Native Americans played in the nation's past.

One textbook had this to say: ". . . he showed a stolid stupidity that no white man could match." Native Americans of all nations were described with one word: "savages." Fierce battles, treachery, and bloody massacres by Native Americans framed the typical textbook account of the past. Few books celebrated the contributions made to the American culture by native people—their

School for African American students in Georgia.
Courtesy of the Library of Congress, Prints & Photographs Division,
LC-USF34-046582-E

religions, arts, music, and legends. Children who learned these "facts" in school could become adults with distorted views of Native Americans.

The 500,000 migrant kids who traveled from place to place with their parents during the 1930s were lucky to attend school at all. The growing seasons dictated their schedules. Work for the parents was more important than school for the kids. Some kids had to work too, so they couldn't go to school.

Cities and towns offered public grammar schools for kids starting at the age of five. High schools were available. Often constructed of brick, they rose two to three stories. City schools usually had electricity, indoor plumbing, and central heating. Many had auditoriums with stages and balconies. They had lunchrooms and sports facilities.

Although city and town schools offered more educational and athletic opportunities as well as more attractive facilities, students were not always satisfied. In Connecticut in 1939 students went on strike. They wanted a shorter school day. During a meeting with the superintendent they booed and hissed as he tried to speak. The striking students carried signs: 8 AM TO 1 PM CLASSES. As they marched they shouted, "We want shorter hours!"

People were divided over the benefits of city versus rural schools. Many rural residents resisted moves to combine one-room schools into

larger buildings with more students and teachers. They believed the rural schools offered a sense of community that would be lacking in larger schools. Others sang the praises of city schools where students were offered more courses, athletics, and social activities. Some thought the academic standards were higher in the larger institutions.

AN ENEMY DIFFICULT TO DEFEAT

NEMESIS

Spelled "n-e-m-e-s-i-s"

The word that caused MacNolia Cox to be eliminated from the National Spelling Bee in 1936. MacNolia was 13 years old when she won the Akron, Ohio, district bee, which meant she received $25 and advanced to the finals in Washington, DC. What an honor for any student! It was especially exciting for MacNolia because she was the first African American to go to the finals.

At the national competition MacNolia did quite well—until a judge gave her the word "nemesis." It was a word that MacNolia couldn't spell. A word that MacNolia didn't remember seeing on the list of approved words for the bee. Sadly, she sat down as the competition continued without her.

The winner that year was Jean Trowbridge, who correctly spelled the word "predilection." A newspaper described her as "very pretty with blond waved bobbed hair."

Some people believed that the word "nemesis" was given to MacNolia by a judge who knew it wasn't one of the preapproved words. Maybe he wanted the first African American girl at the bee to fail. If that was true, it was fitting in some ways. The word "nemesis" means "an opponent or enemy that is very difficult to defeat."

Racism was a nemesis for MacNolia Cox.

Migrant children had few opportunities to attend school.

ger hire kids for low wages. Laws requiring kids under 16 to be in school meant there would be thousands of new students entering the nation's schools. The high rate of unemployment brought on by the Great Depression meant more kids were enrolling in high school because they couldn't get jobs.

Some of President Roosevelt's New Deal programs were designed to keep young people in school. The National Youth Administration (NYA) provided jobs for young people whose families were on relief and for needy high school and college students. Established in June 1935, the NYA trained young people between the ages of 18 and 25 who were not in college as bakers, carpenters, masons, bricklayers, and plumbers. They helped rebuild America's roads, schools, parks, and bridges. High school students in the NYA could work up to three hours per day during the week and seven hours on Saturdays. They earned up to $6 per month as office clerks, assistant librarians, café workers, and museum guides. A high school boy was employed to help new immigrants complete citizenship applications. A girl from a rural area worked as a helper in a girls' 4-H club. Another NYA participant had a job working with newsboys and girls who sold papers on city streets.

Eighteen-year-old John LaRiviere of Haverhill, Massachusetts, had been forced to leave

Both rural and urban schools faced problems brought on by the Great Depression. Their budgets shrank, but the number of students did not decrease. New laws that were intended to reduce or eliminate child labor affected schools. Federal programs encouraged young people to stay in school while working.

New laws that required minimum wages for workers meant business owners could no lon-

high school in his junior year. He wanted to get a job so he could help his father support their family of eight. He was lucky to get a position with the NYA as a patrol officer along the coast. John saved as much as he could from his NYA job; after giving his dad part of this paycheck, he was able to buy parts of broken-down bicycles. He built complete bikes from the salvaged parts and rented the bikes out to customers for 10 cents per hour.

Some New Deal programs were open only to men. Some discriminated against black men and women. Women and girls were included in the NYA because of the determination of First Lady Eleanor Roosevelt. And African Americas were given equal opportunities in the program largely because Mary McLeod Bethune, an African American woman who oversaw the Division of Negro Affairs, ensured they were not excluded.

School leaders worried about the increasing role schools were expected to take in a world where young people worked less and learned more. They saw smaller budgets and bigger classes. But the opportunity to stay in school and get an education opened up new worlds to young people.

A high school in Fullerton, California.
Courtesy of the Library of Congress, Prints & Photographs Division, LC-DIG-fsa-8b31880

KIDS at WORK

TEACHERS IN Lynn, Massachusetts, in the fall of 1934 complained that some of their grammar school students couldn't stay awake during lessons. An inquiry revealed the eight-year-olds were working until midnight for manufacturers of handbags and pocketbooks. They were paid 7 cents an hour.

In Pennsylvania teenage workers in a shirt factory walked off their jobs in May 1933. They thought they were worth more than the 57 cents per week that they were paid.

Kids of all ages worked in factories, stores, and mills during the 1930s. Families needed the money the kids brought into the household. Businesses liked to hire young workers because they could pay them lower wages.

Child labor had been a controversial issue for Americans for many years. In 1916 and 1918 Congress had passed laws restricting child labor. The Supreme Court had declared both unconstitutional. In 1924 Congress passed an amendment to the Constitution limiting the work of children. But for an amendment to become law, it had to be ratified or approved by two-thirds of the states. The amendment never was approved by enough states.

So in the 1930s many children were working at strenuous and dangerous jobs. President Roosevelt opposed child labor, saying, "a self-respecting democracy can plead no justification for the existence of child labor." The president tried to address the problem with his New Deal programs. He took a dramatic step in hiring the first woman to head the Department of Labor. Frances Perkins had numerous qualities that the president admired. But foremost was her determination to wipe out child labor.

Frances knew that too many children were working too many hours in America in the 1930s. She set out to show the public just how serious the problem was. As secretary of the Department of Labor she directed her staff to conduct a survey. They interviewed 449 kids in several states and learned some disturbing facts. About one-quarter of the kids said they worked 60 hours or longer per week. And their wages were around $4 per week.

In 1933 President Roosevelt, with the help of Frances Perkins and others in his administration, tried again to pass a federal law that would limit child labor. He felt he had succeeded when the National Industrial Recovery Act (NIRA) became law. It limited the use of children in businesses and prohibited the labor of children under 16. But the NIRA was overturned by the Supreme Court.

In 1938 another act dealing with child labor was passed. It was successful in making a long-lasting impact on kids in the workplace. It is still in effect. The Fair Labor Standards Act of 1938 limited work for kids under 16. It also specified that kids under 18 couldn't work in hazardous jobs.

Although the Fair Labor Standards Act of 1938 set a minimum working age at 16, there were exceptions—farm kids, for one. And most had to work very hard. In the 1930s farms were family businesses. Everyone in the family contributed. Migrant workers' kids were also excluded from the new law.

Children began working on the farm at a young age gathering eggs, weeding gardens, and caring for animals. Their chores changed as they grew older. Teens milked cows, drove teams of horses or tractors, planted, and harvested big fields of crops.

Farm chores were usually divided by gender. Boys helped their dads in the barn and the fields. Girls worked in the house cleaning, cooking, canning and preserving, laundering, and tending younger siblings. But sometimes everyone helped where they were needed.

Butchering animals for food required many hands. Chickens, cattle, and hogs were raised for food. Usually the family processed the meat and preserved it by canning or pickling. During the Depression, when every morsel was precious, all parts of the animals were used. Scraps were made into sausage. Pickled pigs' feet were a treat. Head cheese couldn't be beat for its delectable flavor. Lard was rendered for shortening in pies

Children working in a potato field in Minnesota.
Courtesy of the Library of Congress, Prints & Photographs Division.
LC-DIG-fsa-8a22232

and for frying meats. Bacon grease was spread on bread in place of butter.

At mealtime farm tables were heaped with food. But that didn't mean anyone wasted anything. Parents admonished kids to "Take only what you can eat." If there were leftovers, they were kept and eaten the next day.

Water was precious too—especially during the "dirty thirties" when many states suffered from drought conditions. Baths were taken once a week. Every drop of water was "recycled." It was customary for the youngest child to get the first bath. After all the kids had bathed, the parents took their turns. The reasoning behind this process was that dad was the dirtiest, so he had the last turn at the water.

On Saturday nights farm families headed to the nearest small town. There the stores stayed open late. There might be performers at the opera house. The community band held concerts in the band shell.

Farmers took goods to town to sell or trade. Women traded eggs, cream, or butter at the store for flour and salt. They picked up feed for their chickens. It came in pretty cotton sacks, and women selected the bags carefully, trying to find several with the same design. The sacks were used to make clothes for the younger children. It was common to see little girls wearing flowered cotton dresses made from chicken feed sacks.

Today when people who survived the Great Depression talk about their years on the farm, many recall good times. They remember that most farm families struggled and were poor, but because they grew food and raised animals, they always had plenty to eat.

However, many farmers ended up losing their farms when the prices they got for their crops and livestock were extremely low. They left the farms to find jobs in town. Some headed to western states hoping to find work. Their children grew up to be adults with sad memories of the 1930s.

POOR EATING LEADS to HEALTH PROBLEMS

GRAVY MADE with bacon grease, flour, and water. Baked bean sandwiches. Salted cow's stomach from a can.

All were common fare at mealtime for some families during the Great Depression. Maybe they don't sound appealing today, but many kids in the 1930s were grateful for every meal. There were no guarantees that there would be three meals per day served in some homes. Many kids went to school hungry.

In 1934 a teacher at Public School 36 in Brooklyn, New York, was fired for giving needy children food in the lunchroom. It wasn't the first time Sylvia Ettinger had served children without lunch tickets. Officials were outraged because after the poor children were served, there wasn't enough food left for the children who had purchased tickets.

"I allowed needy children to eat because I felt their physical conditions warranted free lunches. Most were underweight and suffering from malnutrition," Miss Ettinger explained.

Some families were more fortunate than others. If at least one parent had a job, mealtime was more pleasant. But most families had to be very careful managing the food budget.

"I never knew there were so many different ways to serve potatoes. We had meat . . . but not all through the week," one man recalled.

Despite the hard times, kids had special treats—but not as frequently as they would have liked. "In summer we had one ice cream cone a week instead of one every day," he explained.

In Boston, Massachusetts, schoolkids were lucky. Through donations made by concerned citizens, free lunches were served. Teachers in the city's schools donated percentages of their salaries. An estimated 35,000 meals a day were served to schoolchildren.

Teachers knew vacation times were hard on kids who had little food at home. So over Christmas and Easter holidays some teachers volunteered to offer meals at their schools. One teacher said she wasn't sure what her students did on the weekends when the schools were closed. "But they're always pretty hungry on Mondays," she noted.

When a principal in an Ohio school opened lunchboxes to see what her students were bringing for their lunches, she was shocked and disappointed. Cold boiled potatoes, boiled cabbage, or a "hard biscuit with a slice of fried potato tucked in to make a sandwich" was what

Migrant family in back of truck.
Courtesy of the Library of Congress, Prints & Photographs Division, LC-USF33-012311-M3

she found. When the word got out, church and civic groups teamed up to can fruits and vegetables for school lunches. The Boy Scouts gathered jars and lids from anyone who could spare a few.

Despite the compassion of generous adults, many children suffered from poor nutrition

DEVISE A TREASURE HUNT

BOY AND GIRL SCOUTING was popular during the 1930s. The groups performed community service by distributing food, making toys, and doing good deeds. They also had time for fun. In the January 1934 issue of *Scouting* magazine, a leader described a "Troop Treasure Hunt" he devised. He sent the kids around the city searching for clues. Here are some examples:

CLUE #1: Replace dashes with letters to decipher the sentences.

F–ll–w s––e–m ––w––– –e––essee.
L––k be–e––h – w–––e– b–i––e.

Answer: Follow stream toward Tennessee. Look beneath a wooden bridge.

CLUE #2: Unscramble this coded message:

Lley sderdnuh erehw
Eiv setelhta dna
Hcae denimreted
Eid ro od ot

Answer: Each word and line is written backward. The message wasn't obvious; the boys had to figure out that a place where "hundreds yell" and "athletes vie" referred to the school athletic field.

Where hundreds yell
And athletes vie
Determined each
To do or die

Create a scavenger hunt for your friends. First plan the route. (Write it down so you remember it, but don't let your friends see it.) Then write out the clues, and be creative! This is where you can use your inventiveness. Use the 1934 clues as samples, but take the opportunity to try to stump your friends. The 1934 Scout leader gave his troop three hours to complete the hunt. But no one had arrived at his house (the final stop of the hunt) at the end of the time. One group called to say its members had been puzzling over one of the clues for an hour and a half and needed more time!

Your final clue leads the kids to a location—a house, park, or recreation center—where they enjoy music, games, and refreshments. (You'll need adults to help with this.) The 1934 Boy Scouts' "treasure" was winning points in a competition. Your friends' "treasure" is a party!

during the Great Depression. And as the Depression wore on, year after year, children's health began to suffer.

"It is common to see children who are not more than four with a set of teeth undermined by decay," a dentist at a Los Angeles free clinic stated in 1937.

"For the past seven or eight years underprivileged mothers and children have not been getting the fresh vegetables and fruit they need to build good teeth. That is the principal reason for this condition," he proclaimed.

Long before 1937, health care professionals and educators had been concerned about the effects of poor economic conditions on the health of children. Early in the Great Depression Boston school officials understood they had to do something to help hungry children learn better. They believed the solution was to offer young students extra rest periods and additional meals.

Special nutrition classes were set up. All students began the day at 9 AM. At 10 the students in the nutrition classes went to a "rest room" supplied with cots where they lay down for half an hour. Before rejoining their classmates, they enjoyed milk and a bread-and-butter sandwich. At noon students left for the day, but the nutrition classes stayed for a healthy lunch. Afterward, they took another nap until leaving at 2:30 PM armed with a banana as they headed for home.

In 1934 a survey conducted by the Society for the Prevention of Cruelty to Children showed the "effects of the last four years" had been "devastating and far reaching." The number of kids suffering from hunger, cold, and physical neglect had gone up 37 percent.

The American Association of Social Workers directed a survey of the relief situation in 28 states. One startling finding was related to migrant children. It found that 27 of 30 children of Dust Bowl migrant parents living in a San Joaquin, California, camp were malnourished.

Researchers at the University of Vermont uncovered another surprising situation. Farm children in some areas were suffering more than city kids from poor nutrition. According to the study, only 77 percent of the farm kids consumed a quart of milk each day. Only half of the kids ate two vegetables (not including potatoes) per day. And very few ate any fruit.

DON'T LET the CHILDREN KNOW

"WE DIDN'T realize we were doing without," an adult survivor of the Great Depression recalled 60 years after the hard times had ended.

Her parents had done a superb job of protecting their children from the harsh conditions of the times. Many parents tried to shield their children from their financial woes.

SLANG OF THE 1930S

THE 1930s were a bleak and cheerless time in many ways. Despite the despair that permeated many aspects of life, people held onto their sense of humor and infused it into their everyday lives. One way they showed their lighter side was through their use of slang. Kids supplied many of the witty expressions. Some are still used today. Others were unique to the era and have faded into history.

Some are easy to understand:
"You're the top!"
"He's swell!"
"Scram!"

Others need some explanation:
"Frog skins" = money
"Dead above the shoulders" or "wrong under the hat" = not of sound mind
"Slip me five" = shake my hand

Donald B. Willard, a reporter for the *Daily Boston Globe*, was curious about the meaning of some of the slang he had been hearing coming from the mouths of grammar school boys in the 1930s. So he went to a school and interviewed a group of 12- and 13-year-old students. Here's what he learned:

"Barn rats" were boy gangs.
"Oh, yeah!" A common retort that was not allowed in their school. "Oh, yes" was considered proper.
"Go bag your head," "Get off the air," and "Stick a bun in your mouth" were all something a kid would tell another who talked too much.
"Cheese it, the moose!" meant "Flee! The police are coming."
"Give me a dozen fleas' knees," told to a boastful person—meaning "be quiet and stop bragging."

DEVELOP A SLANG GLOSSARY

EVERY GENERATION develops words that have special meanings. Some of those expressions stand the test of time. Others disappear from the language. Develop a glossary of slang. Who knows? Your new expressions may spread beyond your community, and kids in future generations may be using them in their everyday interactions!

You'll Need

- **Large piece of poster paper**
- **Markers**

Here are a few examples of potential new slang words: sunglasses = rayblockers; door = closer; decorations = dazzlers; bicycles = mobiles.

Begin by brainstorming. Try to think of objects, places, or people that you can develop new words for. Think of the distinct features they have. Write down those characteristics on a large sheet of poster paper. Then think of words or phrases that represent those characteristics.

For example, in the 1930s kids called money "frog skins." Why? Well, a frog's skin is green, and so is money. The characteristic that both frogs and money have is the color green.

Above is a list to get you started.

Share your new slang vocabulary with friends and use it when you talk to or text one another.

Word/phrase	Characteristics	Slang version
Jump rope	long, skinny, wiggly, handles at each end, flips over a jumper's head, snake-like	"snake skin"
Electronic devices		
A favorite friend		
Brother and sister		
A long day at school		
Skateboard		
Video game		
Math class		
Leave me alone		
I like that!		

One dad proudly recalled, "We avoided pessimism at the dinner table. The prime goal was keeping the children contented and happy."

Educators and social workers as well as parents realized that children could be scarred by the frightening realities of such drastic economic times. Some warned children could become "anti-social" or develop "feelings of inferiority." Others feared children's lives would be "warped" or "completely ruined."

Civic and education leaders in the city of Minneapolis, Minnesota, worked together to develop programs to help children cope with the challenges brought on by the Great Depression. The school superintendent said the word "depression" should never be spoken in the classrooms.

"We are trying in every way to keep our children from even *thoughts* of the present economic stress," he said. "We are keeping them so busy with constructive thinking that they have no time to worry about their parents' difficulties."

A social worker with the Family Welfare Agency advised, "Children have to be warned not to ridicule or taunt their playmates whose fathers are out of jobs and whose families have to move to smaller houses, wear made-over clothing, and give up luxuries."

Children of the Great Depression became adults with vivid memories of their experiences. Some memories were painful: Days with little food. Ragged clothes. Worried parents. Many children who lived through the Great Depression became adults who were very thrifty. They were careful not to waste anything. They appreciated their jobs. Some children were lucky to have adults in their lives who shielded them from the unpleasantness of a dark time. Their parents believed it was best to follow this advice: "Don't let the children know."

Pack horse librarian delivers books to hungry readers.

HELPING HANDS
and a "NEW DEAL" AWAKEN HOPE

When Herbert Hoover was president, from 1928 to 1933, most Americans were disappointed that he didn't do more to help those in need. When Franklin Roosevelt became president in 1933, he wanted Americans to know that he was breaking away from the ways of President Hoover. He planned to offer a helping hand and renewed hope for those in America's cities and rural areas. He was offering them a "New Deal"—a new way of getting people back to work out of the Great Depression. As soon as he took office he started programs that would give direct aid to those who needed it.

THE TVA LEADS the WAY to a NEW DEAL for AMERICA

SHE WAS known as a real "firecracker." Some people referred to her as "a red-haired dynamo." Her friends called her "Topie."

Most people in Tennessee didn't know Mary Utopia Rothrock by name, but they couldn't get enough of the precious goods she delivered to their communities. They gobbled them up like chocolate candies.

As in many parts of the United States, people in Tennessee were hungry during the 1930s. They lacked healthy food, and they craved food for their minds too. But buying newspapers, magazines, and books was out of the question for many Tennesseans during the Great Depression.

In 1933 the New Deal program called the Tennessee Valley Authority (TVA), which delivered food for starving bodies and reading materials for hungry minds, began. Parts of Tennessee, Illinois, Kentucky, North Carolina, Georgia, Alabama, and Mississippi benefited from the TVA. Flood control and other conservation projects were part of the program. Farmers learned new ways to control erosion. Dams and power plants were constructed. Residents had electricity for the first time.

Within a year the TVA turned to the task of feeding people's minds. Mary Utopia Rothrock had a reputation for being a forceful librarian.

The TVA hired Mary to oversee a library system. Her job was to supply workers and their families with reading materials. The TVA libraries cropped up in unusual spots—a corner in a country store, shelves in a post office, or a table in a gas station. Everyone loved the idea of borrowing books.

PROVING POVERTY

ORGANIZATIONS SUCH as the Red Cross and the Salvation Army stepped up to help needy people. The Red Cross distributed food and clothing. Its volunteers helped preserve fruits and vegetables for the needy. In Oklahoma City the Salvation Army distributed bags of leftover food from restaurants to homeless families. Salvation Army missions, known as "sallys," offered meals and beds to homeless people.

Goodwill was a refuge for people during the Great Depression. It accepted donations of clothing and household items and then resold them at reasonable prices. In Wisconsin, Goodwill teamed up with the Red Cross to deliver food and clothing. Hundreds of men and women found temporary employment with the agency. In Chicago it opened a school of occupational therapy.

During the Depression years, Goodwill was grateful for any donations. People dropped their unwanted items into bins at Goodwill centers. One day in the mid-1930s workers at a Boston drop-off center discovered a painting in a bin. One of the workers was an artist, and he recognized the painting as one of a very famous 15th-century artist—Gentile Bellini. It was valued at $20,000—a very hefty sum in the 1930s. The Boston Museum of Fine Arts was happy to purchase the painting from Goodwill. When a newspaper reported the story, the owner of the painting contacted the museum. Surely Goodwill would have to return the money. But when the owner of the painting arrived at the Goodwill center, she was so impressed with the work done there that she let the agency keep the $20,000!

Although the federal government was slow in offering programs, city, county, and state governments tried to give relief. In Brooklyn, New York, the city sponsored a program that allowed people to send their leftovers to a central location where hungry people could apply for portions. In New Jersey the rich were encouraged to give their garbage to the hungry.

Often the poor and unemployed had to apply for these handouts. And it wasn't easy to qualify. Before a family could apply, the family had to prove that they truly were desperate. They were required to show that they had no relatives who could help. They had to sell all their possessions and use the money before they could apply for aid. Some cities would not help unmarried or

PACK HORSE LIBRARIANS

AS NOVA KINNARD MADE HER WAY up the rocky bed of Big Laurel Creek in Kentucky, cabin doors swung open and the occupants ran out to greet her. Nova was a pack horse librarian bringing books to people living in remote areas through the Works Progress Administration's Pack Horse Library Service, a New Deal program that operated from 1935 to 1943.

The program gave jobs to people who needed work. It paid salaries but nothing else. It was up to volunteers to acquire

Pack horse librarian delivers books to hungry readers. National Archives (69-N-12581C)

books. After mending and sorting the books and magazines that were donated, the librarians packed them into feed bags or saddlebags and slung them over the horse's back.

The librarian, atop a horse or mule, stopped at stations along the route where books were stored. The librarians dropped off books and magazines and picked some up to take to homes and schools up the road. All sorts of materials were popular. Medical books, Bibles, and novels were eagerly anticipated. When the women gave the librarians their favorite recipes, they were compiled into scrapbooks, and those were added to the library.

Pack horse librarians traveled about 80 miles per week and were paid $28. They had jobs unlike any other librarians, but the people of Kentucky cherished the librarians who arrived at their doorsteps on horseback.

childless individuals. Other cities wouldn't allow people on welfare to vote. Some schools and even churches wouldn't accept people who were getting public assistance.

BUILD A LITTLE LIBRARY

DURING THE GREAT DEPRESSION, families were delighted with the idea that they could get free reading material. Book exchanges remain popular today. Free libraries are set up in public locations or even front yards where anyone can pick up a book and bring another to share with other book lovers. Construct a library out of recycled materials for a spot inside a public building. Fill it with books that you want to pass on to others. As people would have done during the Great Depression, try to use materials you have at home so this activity will cost nothing to complete.

Adult supervision required

You'll Need

- Large box with a cover (A box that holds reams of 8½ by 11-inch (216 by 279-millimeter) paper works well. The box should be big enough to hold at least 20 books.)
- Wrapping paper in a solid color
- Cellophane tape, both two-sided and one-sided
- Two pieces of cardboard big enough to form a peaked roof on the box
- Strong wide tape, like duct tape
- Markers
- Colored construction paper

1. Choose a location for your library. Ask a person in authority for permission to place the library in a store, restaurant, senior center, office building, hospital, mall, or other facility where many people will have access.

2. Wrap the box and lid in solid-color wrapping paper. Use two-sided tape to secure the seams.

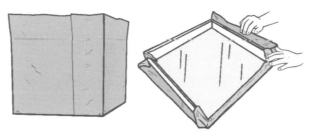

3. Use stiff cardboard to form the roof. Butt two pieces up to each other. Use duct tape to tape them together. Turn over and tape the other side. The two pieces should bend easily at the duct tape seam.

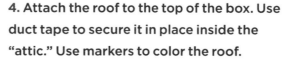

4. Attach the roof to the top of the box. Use duct tape to secure it in place inside the "attic." Use markers to color the roof.

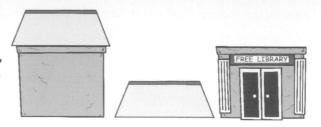

5. Use colored paper and markers to add architectural details such as columns, trim, windows, doors, etc.

6. Include a sign that identifies the "structure" as a free library.

7. On a sheet of paper, write out instructions that explain how to use the library. (For example: Bring a book and take one.)

8. Fill the library with books you would like to donate.

9. Revisit with your contact from step 1. Drop off the library at the location.

10. Revisit the library frequently to make sure there are always books in the box.

In Harlem, New York, a black minister named Father Divine offered relief to needy people at his Peace Mission. He fed thousands. His missions operated businesses such as grocery stores, gas stations, hotels, clothing stores, and restaurants. His businesses offered products and services at prices many people could afford. They also provided jobs. He expanded beyond Harlem and had about 150 missions around the country.

NEIGHBORS HELPING NEIGHBORS

AS THE troubles brought on by the dire economic conditions expanded, more and more city dwellers and farm families watched their friends and neighbors lose their homes. Many people felt hopeless.

Government leaders and banks were viewed as the enemy. It was especially chilling when the local bank foreclosed on a farmer or homeowner. When this happened, people realized that no one was safe and secure. Anyone could lose a job, and the bank could push any family out of its home. It was occurring all around the neighborhoods and farm communities.

It was common for neighbors to share food and clothing as hard times hit families. City dwellers planted community gardens and learned to preserve the produce. Community groups ran soup kitchens where unemployed men could get hot meals. Rural communities made sure kids got shoes and clothes and even a toy for a birthday or holiday.

Caring neighbors invented a clever way to save family farms when banks tried to foreclose on farmers who couldn't pay their mortgages. On the day the bank conducted the auction to sell off the farmer's tools, machinery, and livestock, neighbors gathered at the sale. As the auctioneer asked for an opening bid on the first item, a neighbor shouted out an outrageously low figure. A dime for a plow. A nickel for a cow. A penny for a chicken. All the other neighbors remained quiet. No one bid. If someone did call out another price, people quickly informed the bidder in a low voice that it would be wise to keep quiet. As time ticked away and there were no additional bids, the banker was forced to accept the ridiculously low prices. Then the neighbors, who had paid the low sums, gave everything back to the struggling farmer. These became known as penny auctions.

When people needed help, it was often neighbors who offered hope.

NEW DEAL PROGRAMS OFFER HOPE to MANY

WITHIN THE first 100 days of Franklin Roosevelt's presidency, he signed 15 laws that had been passed by Congress. They were intended to strengthen the banks and businesses, but they also gave aid to the average American.

One of the president's first actions was to declare a bank holiday. It was like a cooling off period. For four days, every bank in the country shut its doors. In a *Fireside Chat* over the radio, President Roosevelt assured Americans that only financially sound banks would reopen. Soon after this, Congress passed a law that established the Federal Deposit Insurance Corporation (FDIC). It meant depositors' accounts were insured—giving Americans confidence to put their money in banks again.

The Agricultural Adjustment Act of 1933 (AAA) made changes for the nation's farmers. It provided aid and regulated crop and livestock production to help them get better prices for their products. But the methods used to get higher prices seemed very peculiar to many.

It involved plowing under fields of crops and killing pigs. Government leaders who understood how a healthy economy worked knew that low supplies of products brought high prices. So if farmers grew fewer crops and raised less livestock, prices should go up. Some crops had already been planted, so government leaders asked farmers to destroy the crops. The government paid farmers to do this. Same with the pigs. In order to have a smaller number of pigs on the market, farmers destroyed many pigs. With fewer hogs around, the price

farmers got for their remaining livestock was greater. But plenty of people were upset about wasting meat and crops at a time when so many people needed food. (Later, a program called the Drought Relief Services allowed the government to *purchase* livestock and cotton from farmers so nothing was wasted. Instead, the livestock and cotton provided food and clothing to needy families.)

There were other problems associated with the AAA. It was intended to help farm owners. Many other people who worked in the agriculture industry needed help too. Sharecroppers and tenant farmers were in terrible shape as a result of the Depression. They did not benefit from the AAA. They felt left out of the New Deal.

President Roosevelt and other government officials knew the AAA had overlooked some farmers. So they hoped a second AAA passed in 1938 would make life better for all farm families. Additional farm programs were created. Small farm owners, tenant farmers, and sharecroppers were included in some of the new programs. The Resettlement Administration offered loans to small farmers to buy land. It provided training to farm families. The Farm Security Administration (FSA) was created to help migrant workers and farmers who rented land.

With millions of Americans out of work, the president knew one of his first tasks was to create jobs. He signed a law that created the Civilian Conservation Corps (CCC). Men between the ages of 18 and 25 joined. These bands of workers lived in camps where they received clothes, a place to live, and three meals per day—something many had not experienced in years. They were given training in the skills they would need to complete their tasks. CCC members earned $30 per month. Most of the money was sent directly to their families, but the workers each kept $5. They worked hard and accomplished much. The CCC built bridges, planted trees, constructed museums, restored historic monuments, and improved parks. Evidence of their work can still be seen across the country today.

The CCC did not include women, yet many women were unemployed. First Lady Eleanor Roosevelt was concerned for all the unemployed women in the country. So she decided to do something for them. She began with an experiment in Bear Mountain State Park near Hyde Park, New York, in June 1933. Seventeen unemployed women from New York City were recruited to participate in the experimental camp. It was called Camp TERA (Temporary Emergency Relief Administration). It gave the women an opportunity to relax and to learn skills.

By 1936 there were 90 camps around the country. Each one was a little different. Some

CCC boys at work in Maryland.
Courtesy of the Library of Congress, Prints & Photographs Division, LC-USF33-T01-000051-M5

A camp for unemployed women.

they were nothing more than government-sponsored vacations. Some called them "She-She-She Camps"—mocking their similarity to the CCC camps. And some Americans believed that the political discussions were infiltrated by Communists.

By October 1937 all the camps were closed. But over 8,000 women had participated.

The Federal Emergency Relief Administration (FERA) was set up to give immediate aid to the people who had been most seriously affected by the Depression. Millions of dollars' worth of food and clothing were distributed to the unemployed, older people, and children. In addition, the Civil Works Administration (CWA) quickly provided jobs for the unemployed. The CWA lasted just for the winter of 1933–34. About four million workers built roads, bridges, schools, playgrounds, and airports.

President Roosevelt expanded the Reconstruction Finance Corporation (RFC) that President Hoover had formed. He increased funding for the agency and used it to support key industries such as banks and railroads. The RFC gave loans to every state for relief efforts.

The New Deal set up the Public Works Administration in 1933. It designed public works projects that created jobs and stimulated business. Over a six-year period money was used to build dams, aircraft carriers, schools, and

offered more vacation-like experiences, while others provided training in job skills. Some of the camp directors encouraged the women to engage in lively discussions. Often they were political in nature. In fact, that was exactly what Mrs. Roosevelt envisioned when she started the camps—opportunities for young women to relax, learn, and expand their experiences.

Many Americans refused to take the camps for unemployed women seriously. They said

hospitals. Housing projects were built to offer clean, safe homes at affordable prices.

The Homeowners Loan Corporation made mortgage loans to people who wanted to buy homes. It also helped people who already had mortgages and were about to lose their homes.

In 1935 the Works Progress Administration (WPA) was created. It was a work program that employed 8.5 million between 1935 and 1943. The jobs put people to work building highways, roads, streets, bridges, public buildings, parks, recreation facilities, and schools. People were hired to read to the blind, work as home health aides, and care for children in nurseries. However, more than one facet of the WPA became controversial.

The *Daily Boston Globe* caught the attention of readers with this headline: "Schools for Maids to Cost $500,000." It reported that the WPA was spending the money to train maids "to serve the soup and dust the furniture correctly." Women who were selected for the slots would receive uniforms and $1 per day for car fare while in training. At the end of the course, successful students would receive certificates of proficiency and help with job placement.

Despite news reports that sensationalized the schools for maids, thousands of women enrolled across the country. In Spokane, Washington, women who completed the course found positions that paid $30 per month.

A NEW DEAL for the ARTS

FEDERAL PROJECT Number One—also known as Federal One—established programs that helped unemployed artists, writers, musicians, and actors. In addition, young people who were interested in those professions received training. Federal One introduced culture into communities across the nation. At the same time valuable cultural artifacts were created and restored.

The Federal Art Project hired painters and sculptors to create art for public spaces. Many showed scenes of people working. It sponsored traveling art exhibits—giving Depression-weary Americans a respite from their troubles. Murals depicting everyday life were designed and painted on post offices across the country. Many of these still exist. Community art centers were established, giving residents of towns and rural areas opportunities to appreciate various art forms. Graphic designers were put to work creating posters that advertised some of the new government programs.

The Federal Writers' Project (FWP) gave unemployed writers assignments that produced some priceless gems. The stories of Americans were captured and preserved through oral histories. Interviewers asked questions such as "What do you do for recreation?" "What superstitions do you hold?" "Describe your typical workday." Three hundred writers completed 2,900

Poster promoting the WPA Maids' School.
Courtesy of the Library of Congress, Prints & Photographs Division, LC-USZC2-1500

The Federal Theatre Project offered classes for kids.

biographies over four years. Marie Haggerty from Massachusetts was interviewed about her work as a maid. Clyde "Kingfish" Smith, a New York City street vendor who sold fish, talked about attract-ing buyers by making up rhymes: "Heigh-ho, fish man, bring down your pan."

Writers also produced guidebooks for each state. The books highlighted the history, archi-tecture, and culture of the area. These guides made people realize that although the country was hurting, there was much to be proud of all across the nation.

Through the Federal Music Project commu-nity symphonies and orchestras were formed. Performances of various types were offered—usually free of charge to the public. Instrumental and vocal, choral, chamber music, opera, and dance band performances were given in cities and towns. Musicians were hired and performed in events across the country.

Traveling theater groups and dancers offered entertainment to small and large communities throughout the country through the New Deal's Federal Theatre Project. Money was provided to pay the salaries of actors, stagehands, ush-ers, lighting technicians, and box office work-ers. Plays, circuses, puppet shows, and dramas offered entertainment to a variety of audiences. This federal program invented a very interesting way of spreading the news. The Living News-paper combined current events with art. Artists performed skits about issues that confronted everyday Americans. Health care, education, politics, and consumer problems were all topics that were tackled in an artistic way.

SECURITY for ALL

A LASTING New Deal program that many Americans use today is Social Security. The secretary of labor, Frances Perkins, wanted to set up a program that would ensure older Americans would have money each month so they could retire. And she wanted to offer unemployment insurance to people who lost their jobs. In addition, her idea provided aid to families with dependent children and disabled individuals. After some negotiating, Congress passed the Social Security Act, and the president signed it into law in 1935.

At a time when millions of Americans looked to the federal government for more intervention in their lives, many Native Americans were eager for less. "It is necessary that the Indians themselves discuss their own affairs and set forth their views," said Scott H. Peters, president of the Grand Council Fire of American Indians in the early 1930s. Peters wanted non-Indians—especially government leaders—to stop making decisions for his people. He voiced his thoughts whenever he could. And President Roosevelt heard his comments.

One of the president's New Deal actions was to appoint John Collier as commissioner of Indian Affairs. Scott H. Peters worked with him to find jobs for Native Americans. In 1934 the Indian Reorganization Act was passed by Congress. It returned lands to native people, gave

DESIGN A GUIDE "BOOK" OF YOUR STATE

THE FEDERAL WRITERS' PROJECT paid writers and historians to develop guidebooks for each of the 48 states. (Hawaii and Alaska were not yet states.) They used words and pictures to portray the scenery, history, culture, and natural and economic resources of the states. It was a time when people needed to be reminded of the greatness of America.

You'll Need
- Computer with Internet access
- Pen and paper or a word-processing program
- Other materials, dependent on format (might include bookmaking materials, poster board, markers, camera, video camera, tape recorder, movie-making app, performance space, and so on)

Your guide "book" doesn't have to be in paper format. Include information about your state's history, culture, and natural and economic resources. Many communities have parks, buildings, or structures that were built by the Civilian Conservation Corps. Include them in your guide.

Consider including attractions, famous people, historical sites, interesting facts, and even "weird" facts such as unusual state laws.

1. Look at some of the guides produced in the 1930s at this site: www.digitalbook index.org/_search/search010histus20 fedwriproja.asp.

2. Conduct research on your state. Find other resources that promote the state. What categories are included—the arts, industries, sports, etc.? What format was used by the designers?

3. Make an outline of the key concepts you will include in your guide.

4. Decide the format your guidebook will take—video, slide show, poster (paper or electronic), picture gallery exhibition, dance, performance, etc.

5. Use a variety of images, text, music, video, and interviews to tell the story of your state.

6. Present the product to your school or community. Donate it to the public library.

PERFORM A LIVING NEWSPAPER

THE FEDERAL THEATRE PROJECT used skits to inform audiences about current events. The performers wanted viewers to think about the issues and discuss possible solutions to problems. *One-Third of a Nation* highlights the need for better housing for poor Americans. Script writers included authentic photographs taken in the nation's slums in the production to emphasize the magnitude of the problem. Try your hand at writing and performing your own play script about one of today's pressing issues.

You'll Need
🖎 A news story or series of stories on a topic of concern to many people
🖎 Several friends
🖎 Computer with Internet access
🖎 Video camera or smartphone
🖎 Costumes and props

1. Do online research to help you choose a problem from current headlines. (Example: Is global warming a real problem?)

2. Decide on a setting in which the actors will present the problem and solutions. (For example, the problem is presented when a family gathers for a holiday meal.)

3. Who are the participants? (Grandparents, parents, siblings, cousins, etc.)

4. Write a script that describes the actions and words of each participant. The script should:

🖎 give a detailed description of the setting
🖎 describe the problem
🖎 offer a variety of viewpoints
🖎 propose a solution(s) to the problem.

Use your script as a guide as you perform your Living Newspaper. Ask friends to fill the acting roles. Use props such as photographs and video to enhance your performance. Record the event with a video device.

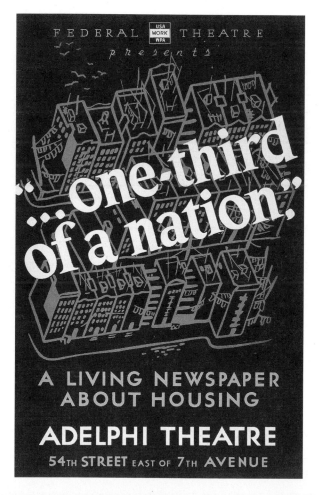

A poster for a Living Newspaper performance about problems with housing in America.
Courtesy of the Library of Congress, Prints & Photographs Division, LC-DIG-ppmsca-31218

them more self-government, and allowed children to attend schools on their reservations.

Some people criticized the New Deal programs. Never before had the federal government become so involved in the lives of everyday citizens. Some people thought it was ridiculous for the Congress and the president to give so much federal money to the states and local communities.

Millions of Americans had lost their homes and farms when the Great Depression hit. Many stood in breadlines for free food. When President Roosevelt proposed spending federal money on bird sanctuaries and fish hatcheries through the Civilian Conservation Corps, there were plenty of people who thought it was a foolish idea. And when federal money went to support the work of actors, writers, artists, and musicians, there were Americans who were outraged. Some people thought these projects were frivolous and unnecessary.

Many Americans saw things differently. They wanted to protect and replenish wildlife for their children and grandchildren. And they wanted to help bring culture to all Americans in their communities. They knew America's history and arts needed to be preserved for future generations.

They were grateful for the role the government played in their lives. It seemed like more positive things occurred than negative. People received

FIRST DAUGHTERS OF AMERICA

"…her eyes they are lit with lightnings
Her heart is not afraid!"
–"From the Land of Sky-blue Water" by Charles Wakefield Cadman

THESE LYRICS ARE FROM A BEAUTIFUL musical composition written about a lovely Indian maiden named Tsianina Blackstone. Tsianina was a gifted composer, pianist, and singer as well as the subject of a song. This Cherokee Creek woman studied music in Denver and New York and sang all over the United States and in Europe. She performed at the New York Metropolitan Opera.

She was unhappy with the images of her people that she saw in movies and schoolbooks. So she decided to bring about change. In 1930 she started a women's club called "First Daughters of America." Its purpose was to help people see Native Americans as producers of cultural artifacts. And she wanted non–Native Americans to see the value of other women like herself.

As the Great Depression deepened for all Americans, Tsianina wanted to help her people. She opened a shop in Chicago where rich people could buy fine artwork and precious objects handmade by Native Americans. It provided jobs and helped non-natives to see natives as valuable contributors to American culture.

Tsianina and the other First Daughters of America fought against the images Americans saw in Wild West shows, movies, and schoolbooks. They hoped to erase words like "lazy savages" and "uncivilized heathens" from the American culture.

the basic goods—food, clothes, a place to live. They even were exposed to cultural events. Most of all they went to work. And for those Americans who hadn't gotten a paycheck in years, a job was priceless.

Shirley Temple leaving the White House.
Courtesy of the Library of Congress, Prints & Photographs Division, LC-DIG-hec-24775

FINDING FUN *in* GLOOMY TIMES

In 1934 the president of the United States created a new cabinet position—Secretary of Amusement—whose job it was to bring the American public out of the doldrums of the Great Depression. Of course this was not a *real* step taken by the president but the plot of a movie released that year. *Stand Up and Cheer* contains 80 minutes of song, dance, and patriotic costumes. One of the acts is a musical number by a six-year-old newcomer named Shirley Temple. "Baby Take a Bow" was a peppy performance audiences loved. It was the first major picture for the little girl, and it propelled her into a career as one of the most celebrated child stars of all time.

Shirley had already been performing for three years by the time *Stand Up and Cheer* was made, but her life was never the same after that performance. She wowed audiences with her singing, dancing, and acting in every one

Circus performer Gene Wallick.
Used with permission from Illinois State University's Special Collections, Milner Library

of her films. Her picture appeared in newspapers and magazines all over the world. The image of a bright-eyed, happy little child was just what Depression Era families needed to give them hope for the future. President Franklin Roosevelt said, "As long as our country has Shirley Temple, we will be all right."

Although there was never a real Secretary of Amusement to cheer Americans, there were plenty of amusements that helped people find fun in these gloomy times.

CIRCUSES LIFT SPIRITS

SCHOOLCHILDREN IN Newburyport, Massachusetts, were undecided about which adult they should obey in May 1931. The mayor, Andrew J. Gillis, also known as "Bossy Gillis," had issued an edict stating that all children should stay out of school on the day the circus came to town. He wanted them to join him for a fun day at the big top. The superintendent of schools, Starr King, insisted it would be "business as usual." Most of the students did as their superintendent suggested but wasted no time getting to the circus after classes ended. When they arrived, they were just in time to see the mayor waving his hat in the air perched atop an elephant.

Although Newburyport's schools did not shut down for the circus in 1931, the arrival of a traveling circus was a cause for celebration in towns across the country throughout the Depression Era. Kids and adults flocked to see the wild animals and daring performers.

Circuses provided hours of fun and release from the gloomy side of life during the Great Depression. They also provided jobs. During good times the circus provided workers with a place to sleep and three meals a day in addition to a salary. However, by the 1930s circuses were not the only show in town. Radio and movies offered tantalizing entertainment as well. Circus attendance began to decline. As the Great Depression deepened, circus owners began to cut back. They laid off workers.

INVISIBLE WORLDS BROUGHT to LIFE by RADIO

"Hello, Pretenders!"

THE COUNTRY was deep into the Great Depression. What better time to pretend?

One of the most popular children's shows on the radio in 1934 was *Let's Pretend*. Each episode featured a well-known fairy tale, and the characters were portrayed by child actors. At the beginning of each show the announcer greeted listeners—in the studio audience and in homes across America—with "Hello, Pretenders!"

Sneaking a peek under the big top. Courtesy of the Library of Congress, Prints & Photographs Division, LC-DIG-fsa-8b27414

Another radio show—one of the most popular of all time—was *Amos 'n' Andy*. It involved pretending too. Two white men, Freeman Gosden and Charles Correll—played the roles of African American men—Amos Jones and Andy H. Brown. Many people found the two characters loveable, but their speech and actions depicted them as ignorant and lazy. The portrayal of black men in this light helped to reinforce stereotypes that were hurtful, harmful, and untrue. Some black leaders wanted the show removed from the airwaves, but they were largely ignored. *Amos 'n' Andy* aired five times a week for 15 minutes, and it seemed the entire nation stopped to listen to a show that many found very humorous.

In the 1930s almost every family in America had a radio—usually situated in a prime spot in the living room. The entire family gathered around the set to listen in the evenings. In 1930, 12 million households had radios; by 1939 the number had risen to 28 million—90 percent of all homes.

While many listeners were laughing over the antics of two white actors pretending to be African Americans in the *Amos 'n' Andy* series, a group of talented black singers were impressing radio audiences with their Negro spirituals. The Wings Over Jordan Choir was popular with white as well as black audiences. In time the program included speakers in addition to music. It offered a stark contrast to the image of black Americans seen in *Amos 'n' Andy*.

Other classic radio shows included *Ripley's Believe It or Not*, featuring weird and unusual people, places, and things from around the world. *The Chase and Sanborn Hour* was a variety show that included a ventriloquist named Edgar Bergen and his wooden dummy named Charlie McCarthy. *Burns and Allen* starred married comedians George Burns and Gracie Allen.

Producers of radio programming knew that kids were a big audience, and they created special programs just for them. *Buck Rogers* was a science fiction show set in the 25th century. *The H-Bar-O Rangers* was a show about a young orphan—Bobby Benson—who inherited a Texas ranch.

AMERICA LOVES the TALKIES

WOGGLES, PETER, and Adolph were dogs who lived better than some humans during the Great Depression. They were movie stars' dogs, and they lived very well.

Woggles, Joan Crawford's black Scotty, snoozed on the pink satin couch in her dressing room. John Barrymore's dog, Peter—who starred with his master in the movie *Moby Dick*—also accompanied the Barrymore family on yachting trips. The debonair Maurice Chevalier led his dog, Adolph, around the movie lot on a jeweled leash.

WRITE AND PERFORM THEN-AND-NOW RADIO SCRIPTS

ALMOST EVERYONE had a radio at home in the 1930s. There were no televisions yet, so the radio was the primary source of electronic information and entertainment. Radios are still important sources of news and music. However, the content today is different in many ways than in the 1930s. In this activity you will compare today with the past.

You'll Need
- Several friends/helpers
- Computer with Internet access
- Word processing program
- Audio recording device
- Objects for sound effects (pans, wooden spoons, running water, rocks in a jar, etc.)
- Music to set the mood

Develop a script for a five-minute segment of a radio program for kids living in the 1930s. Listen to shows from a popular program to get ideas.

Then develop a script for a five-minute radio segment for kids today. Because serials like the Bobby Benson show are not produced today for radio, your segment will consist of music, talk, weather, public service announcements, or news and traffic reports.

Both will require planning:

1930s:
- Identify the characters.
- Where and when does it take place?
- What is the plot? Is there a message you want to convey?
- What sound effects will you use?
- Choose appropriate music that sets the mood.

Current:
- What format will you use? (A combination of music, talk, news, etc.)
- What is your message or messages?
- What music will you play?
- Identify individuals to play announcers/reporters, celebrities, etc.

1. Write both scripts and rehearse them a couple times with your friends.

2. Record both programs and play them for an audience. Watch their expressions as they listen. How did they react?

3. To compare, use a Venn diagram to illustrate similarities and differences. The overlapping area represents the elements that are the same today as in the 1930s. The section labeled "A" represents only the 1930s; "B" represents only today.

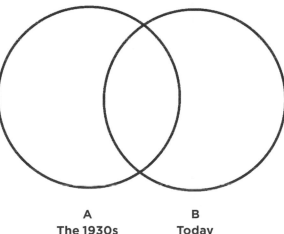

A	B
The 1930s	Today

Because millions of Americans were willing to pay 25 cents for a movie ticket in the 1930s, movie stars and their pets were able to live elaborate lifestyles. In 1932 more than half the population went to the movies at least once a week. There were more movie theaters in the country than banks.

Silent movies had been popular in the 1920s. When new technologies made "talkies" possible in the 1930s, moviegoers couldn't get enough. People went crazy for dramatic, comedy, horror, and musical films with stars like Joan Crawford, John Barrymore, and Maurice Chevalier.

The same year the stock market crashed—1929—the first Academy Awards were held. In the 1930s the best picture awards were given to a variety of film types. *All Quiet on the Western Front* was a drama about the Great War. *Cimarron*, a western, won in 1931. *The Great Ziegfeld*, a three-hour musical, won in 1936. And a romantic historical saga, *Gone with the Wind*, was honored in 1939.

The glamorous stars of the 1930s came to Hollywood from many different places and situations. The handsome and sophisticated celebrity who went by the name Cary Grant was born Archibald Leach and left his home in England at the age of 15. He made his way to Hollywood where he became a sensation in the movies. Clark Gable, a dashing leading man throughout the 1930s, quit school at 16 and worked at a factory before joining a traveling acting troupe. He found his way to Hollywood where he won an Oscar in 1935. Norwegian Sonja Henie was an Olympic figure skating champion who became a popular movie star in the 1930s.

While famous movie stars lived the good life and earned salaries that others could only dream of, the Great Depression also affected the movie industry. In 1933, Hollywood's motion picture producers asked hourly workers to take a pay cut "as a means of weathering the current financial storm." Big-name stars were also expected to see cuts in their salaries. However, no one believed the celebrities would suffer.

CHILD STARS STEAL the SHOWS

Chucky Koontz, "The World's Biggest Little Magician"
Betty Jane Kolar, "The World's Youngest Magician"

CHUCKY WAS 13 years old and Betty Jane only 7 when they were known by these superlatives of the entertainment world. Chucky was a magician and ventriloquist from Pittsburgh, Pennsylvania. He entertained audiences with his magic and dummy acts at schools, hospitals, and conventions. He wrote a regular advice column in a newsletter for ventriloquists called *Double Talk*.

In the May 1938 issue Chucky wrote, "The audience likes to think of your splinter (the wooden dummy) as human, but they also like you to show that you know they are not fooled."

Betty Jane Kolar's parents were pleased with their daughter's aptitude for picking up new skills quickly. Mr. Kolar was a magician and Mrs. Kolar was a mind reader, and they taught Betty Jane everything they knew.

"I'd just as soon have her be a magician as anything else, but I want her to be a good one," Betty Jane's dad remarked.

Betty Jane could read a deck of cards, make an egg disappear and reappear, and—the trick that captivated people of all ages most of all—Betty Jane could pull a live rabbit from a silk hat!

Chucky and Betty Jane were certainly celebrities during the 1930s. However, they were not as well known as the radio and movie child stars of the time. Radio networks and film companies made big names of little children. Shirley Temple and Jackie Cooper were two of the many who became household names.

One day in 1932, 13-year-old Billy Idelson played hooky from his school in a Chicago suburb. He made his way to the NBC radio studios in downtown Chicago, where he had heard auditions were being held for a part in a series that was broadcast on the station. Billy's performance knocked out the competition, and he got the part of Rush in the series *Vic and Sade*. He played the adopted son of Vic and Sade Gook. The series portrayed a typical American family with their ups and downs like any family. In one show Rush was annoyed with Sade for volunteering him to recite this poem at a friend's party: "My baby face is like a flower / my eyes grow bluer every hour."

"Take a look at my 'baby face,' Mom, it's got fuzz on it. In another year I'll be shaving," Rush complained.

A bunch of poor kids with memorable names—Spanky, Alfalfa, Buckwheat, and Porky—captivated moviegoers of all ages in the 1930s. The Our Gang series of short films began as silent productions in the 1920s. The actors who portrayed the kids changed over the years, but enthusiasm for the series prevailed.

Jackie Cooper starred in "Teacher's Pet," "School's Out," and "Love Business"—three programs in the Our Gang series. While making the movies, he earned a whopping $1,300 per week. Other stars included an African American boy—Matthew Beard—who appeared in 36 of the Our Gang shows. Dorothy DeBorba was only five years old when she appeared in her first Our Gang program. In the program titled "Love Business," Dorothy played Chubby's little sister, who had an annoying habit of echoing him as he practiced what he would say to his love—but never getting it quite right. "Darling, can you hear the pleas in my whispers?" Chubby recited.

Betty Jane Kolar hypnotizes a rabbit.
CriticalPast

To which Dorothy mimicked, "Darling, I hear the fleas in your whiskers!"

Frances Gumm sang professionally for the first time when she was only two and a half years old. It was the beginning of a remarkable career in show business. Frances changed her name to Judy Garland and at the age of 13 signed a contract with MGM studios in Hollywood. The movie that made Judy Garland a household name and for which she is always remembered is *The Wizard of Oz*. It gave her an opportunity to showcase her outstanding singing abilities in addition to her acting.

SCHOOLBOY WRITES BLOOD-CURDLING YARN

"THE RANCH CAUGHT ON FIRE and every man ran for his life.... Suddenly the roof fell in and closed down on the fight."

This line is from an action-packed book for kids published in 1938. *Roaring Guns* was a "blood-curdling yarn of bad men" of the Old West. Its pages were chock-full of good guy–bad guy conflicts, shoot-outs, and a little romance. This was not an unusual storyline in novels for young readers in the 1930s. However, the author *was* surprising. David Statler was only eight years old when he wrote and illustrated *Roaring Guns* from his home in Tennessee. His parents had read their son's project and filed it away with other childhood mementos. One day an aunt, who worked at a bookstore, saw David's masterpiece and contacted an agent, who found a New York publishing house to produce the book.

By the time it was published, David was 11 years old. In an interview he admitted he wished he had been a better speller at age eight—the publisher had printed the book in its original version—spelling errors and all. For example: the "badest" (baddest) robber in the book was a man named Bill "Jhonson" (Johnson). And the ranch owner's daughter was "Nomra" (Norma).

David said he was inspired to write the story after watching western movies. He often played cowboys with his brother. These experiences influenced the drawings he included in the book—pencil sketches of stick men.

Roaring Guns ended with the main character riding off into the wilds of Mexico—leading readers to believe there might be a sequel.

BOOKS ARE PRICELESS

CHILDREN AND young adults had plenty of choices when it came to reading. Parents read *Bingo Is My Name* to their toddlers. Bingo is a little dog that becomes jealous when another dog comes to visit. When a bigger dog attacks the visiting pooch, Bingo comes to the rescue of his visitor.

The Ameliaranne series of books introduced older readers to a girl growing up in a large family with little money—something many Depression Era kids understood. Ameliaranne doesn't let her situation hold her down. The series includes *Ameliaranne at the Circus*, *Ameliaranne Camps Out*, and many others.

Adults wanted books that released them from the realities of life during the Great Depression. When a book about hobbits, wizards, and dragons—*The Hobbit*—was published in 1937, it was widely read.

While a fantasy world seemed appealing to many readers, the true-to-life world of a family of sharecroppers looking for a better life in

California was just as absorbing to adult readers. In *The Grapes of Wrath* readers follow the Joad family from Oklahoma to the West during the Dust Bowl. Women who had served in the Great War in France compiled a cookbook—*Approved Enduring Favorites.* Julia Stimson, superintendent of the Army Nurse Corps, submitted "Des Oeufs, And How!"—"The Eggs, And How!"

For those who could afford it, a book could be purchased for 50 cents to $2.50. For others, there was another invaluable source. Public libraries were widely used during the Great Depression. Where else could a family strapped for funds travel to faraway lands and mingle with magical creatures in mystical worlds—all for free? Books were havens for Depression Era families. An editorial in the *New York Times* in 1938 summed up the way many felt: "books are priceless in the joys they bring and the good they do."

SPORTS PREVAIL over ECONOMIC WOES

JACKIE MITCHELL was 17 years old when she was offered a contract with the Lookouts, a minor league baseball team in Chattanooga, Tennessee. (It may have been the first professional baseball contract ever given to a woman.) It was 1931, and America was in love with the sport and its superstars, such as the New York Yankees' big hitters Babe Ruth and Lou Gehrig.

LEARN A MIND-READING TRICK

BETTY JANE KOLAR was a child star in the mind-reading business in the 1930s. Here's a trick to use with friends that will make them believe you are a mind reader.

You'll Need
- About 10 friends
- Slips of paper and pen for each participant
- Container

Before the performance, in secret identify one friend to be the helper. Ask him (or her) to tell you a short sentence—which he will write down on a slip of paper with the other participants shortly. Memorize it.

Gather the friends in a semicircle of chairs about five feet away from the mind reader (you). Ask everyone to write a short, simple sentence on the slip of paper and fold it once. (If your audience is made up of younger kids, ask them to draw a picture of something instead of a sentence and to remember it.) Ask for a helper. Choose the person who is your secret helper. He gathers the papers, puts them in the container, and stands next to you, the mind reader.

The helper randomly selects a slip from the container and holds it (with the writing toward the forehead) to your forehead. You pretend to "read" the message. In reality, you recite (from memory) the sentence that your helper secretly gave you before the performance, "My dog's name is Bingo."

The helper hands you the paper from your forehead and you pretend to "read" it aloud, but you are actually reciting from memory the helper's sentence, "My dog's name is Bingo." The helper verifies that he wrote the sentence "My dog's name is Bingo."

At the same time, you are memorizing the sentence you see on the slip of paper that was pressed to your forehead. You do this so you can "read" it and recite it when the next paper is pressed to your forehead. This process continues until all the sentences have been "read."

It's not mind reading, but it *is* playing mind games with your friends.

Jackie Mitchell.
Underwood and Underwood/Corbis/AP Images

It wasn't unusual for team promoters to stage exhibition games between major and minor league teams before the regular season began. In April 1931 the Yankees were scheduled for games in Chattanooga against the hometown team. They were set to play on April 1, but rain delayed the game until the next day.

On April 2, as the legendary Babe Ruth stepped to the plate, the Lookouts' left-handed female pitcher—Jackie Mitchell—threw the first pitch to the famous hitter. The umpire called, "Ball!" And the next two—"Strike!" "Strike!" The next pitch sailed past Babe, with the umpire calling, "Strike!" The crowd roared. A 17-year-old girl had struck out the Sultan of Swat!

Next up was another celebrity slugger—Lou Gehrig. But it didn't take Jackie long to take care of the renowned hitter known as the Iron Horse, 1-2-3. The balls whizzed past the great Iron Horse as the ump cried, "Strike" three times.

Newspapers carried the story of how a teenage girl struck out two of baseball's greatest hitters. Everyone was talking about it. But maybe it was too good to be true. History has never solved that mystery. The game originally was planned for April Fools' Day. Was it intended to be baseball's greatest trick? Did Babe and Lou play along just to be good sports? No one knows.

Major league baseball continued to fascinate Americans throughout the Depression. Joe DiMaggio was one of many players who captivated the nation. He joined the Yankees in 1936. During that first year, Joe helped the Yankees take the World Series. In 1939 he won the Most Valuable Player (MVP) award.

Many Americans couldn't get enough of professional boxing during the 1930s. Early in the decade Max Baer—Madcap Maxie—was a famous fighter. He grew up working on a cattle ranch in California but turned to professional boxing in 1929. One of his opponents died after being knocked out by Max, and for a time he left boxing. But Madcap Maxie came back, and in 1934 he won the title of heavyweight champion of the world.

Another popular boxer was a black man named Joe Louis. When Joe was 10 years old, his family moved from Alabama to Detroit, Michigan. He started boxing as a youth and became a professional in 1934. Joe's fighting career flourished, and he became known as the Brown Bomber. No one could beat Joe—until 1936. The world was stunned when German Max Schmeling defeated the Brown Bomber. In 1937 Joe won the title of heavyweight champion of the world. But he couldn't forget his defeat by the German. Finally in 1938 Joe met up with Max again. And this time the Brown Bomber won.

Although the Great Depression had a worldwide impact on the economy and disrupted life for many, it failed to spoil a tradition that occurred every four years and that involved athletes from all over the globe. In 1932 the United States hosted both the winter and summer Olympic games. The winter games were held in Lake Placid, New York. Athletes from 17 countries competed in nine sports, including dogsled

Heavyweight champion of the world Joe Louis.
Library of Congress, Prints & Photographs Division, Carl Van Vechten Collection, LC-USZ62-109776

racing. The summer games were held in Los Angeles. The star of the Los Angeles games was a woman named Mildred "Babe" Didrikson. She won two gold medals and a silver in the 80-meter hurdles, javelin, and high jump. The United States won a bronze medal for field hockey, but there were only three countries competing. India and Japan took the gold and silver.

The 1932 Olympics were memorable for two African American track and field athletes. Louise Stokes and Tidye Pickett were stars at their colleges and qualified for the Olympics. On the train trip to Los Angeles from Illinois the US women's track team stopped over in Denver, Colorado, for a night. When the women gathered in the hotel for the evening meal, Louise and Tidye were not with the team. They were not allowed to eat in the dining room because they were black.

When the team reached Los Angeles, the Olympic Committee had a special meeting. When it was over, two white runners who had slower times than Louise and Tidye in the trials had replaced the African American women on the team.

The 1936 winter and summer Olympics were held in Germany. Adolf Hitler was in power and had begun to impose his ideas about a "master race"—the belief that blond-haired, blue-eyed white people were superior to all others. There had been talk of boycotting from some nations because of reports of persecution of Jews in Germany, but the summer games included the highest number of participating countries ever. Forty-nine nations traveled to Germany. The US team was the second largest.

Included in the US team were 18 African Americans. Louise Stokes and Tidye Pickett didn't let their snub at the 1932 games deter them. They both qualified for the 1936 games. Tidye made history when she became the first African American woman to compete in the Olympics. Jesse Owens, the grandson of a slave, performed in track and field. He won four gold medals for the United States.

Another record was set by an American swimmer—Marjorie Gestring. She became the youngest Olympic gold medalist ever when she competed in a diving event at the 1936 Olympics. Marjorie was only 13 years and nine months old.

Sports enthusiasts also followed the celebrated tennis career of Helen Wills Moody throughout the 1920s and '30s. She retired in 1938 after winning her eighth Wimbledon title.

As a young child Alice Marble played baseball and basketball and did a little boxing. At the age of 15 she started playing tennis. She won many junior tennis competitions, but had to retire from the sport for a time for health reasons. But she came back to win the US singles title as well as Wimbledon singles and doubles competitions throughout the late 1930s.

DESIGN A CROSSWORD PUZZLE

CROSSWORD PUZZLES were a very popular form of amusement in the 1920s and '30s. Today they are still popular with adults as well as kids. Design a crossword puzzle that will stump your friends.

You'll Need

- Paper
- Ruler
- Pen or pencil
- Dictionary

Puzzle-Making Hints:

- Long puzzles with many words will be more difficult to solve. Also, your clues should be clever and not too easy.
- You can add interest by including a hidden word. Think about a word that relates to your theme and randomly place circles around some boxes. Each of those will hold one letter of the word. The letters don't have to be in order because the puzzle solver will have to "unscramble" the secret word. Don't forget to include a clue for it.

1. Decide the total grid size (for example, 9 squares by 12 squares). Draw the grid lines on a large sheet of paper.

2. Identify the theme of your puzzle (for example, all words related to airplanes and flying). Give the puzzle a creative title related to the theme (for example, "In the Clouds").

3. Make a list of words associated with the theme. Next to each word, write a clue. This is your design document. Puzzle solvers will not see it.

4. Place the words from your list in the grid. Arrange them horizontally and vertically. Interconnect (or "cross") as many words as possible. Black out the squares that do not contain letters. (This is also a design document.)

5. Assign numbers to each vertical word and each horizontal word. Place the corresponding number in the upper left-hand corner of the letter box of the first letter of each word. Continue until you've used all the words in your list. This is your answer key.

6. Duplicate this grid, leaving the words out. Keep the numbers and the black squares in place.

7. Give the blank puzzle to a friend or family member. Give them the clues sheet. Wish them luck!

In the Clouds

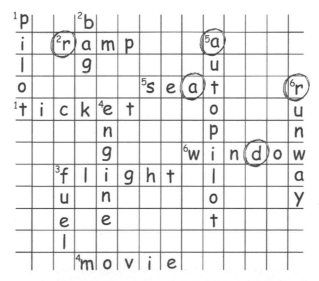

secret word = radar

IGLOO STARTED HIS LIFE as a homeless mutt living on the streets in the nation's capital. But the lucky dog was adopted by one of the world's most admired explorer aviators.

Richard E. Byrd was a superstar of the late 1920s and early '30s. He was believed to be the first person to fly over the North Pole, making the 15½-hour flight from Norway in 1926. Between 1928 and 1941 Byrd led expeditions to Antarctica and the South Pole.

Igloo was only a puppy when he accompanied Byrd on his first Arctic trip. While in Antarctica, Igloo grew a thick fluffy coat. But when temperatures hovered around -60°F, it wasn't enough to keep him warm. So the men made him a wool coat and tiny leather boots.

When Byrd returned from his trips he spent a great deal of time making speeches about his travels. One day in the spring of 1931 he was in Illinois for an appearance. Igloo was at the Byrd home in Boston. Byrd received an urgent call that his beloved pet was seriously ill. He chartered a plane to rush back to Boston, but Igloo could not be saved.

He was buried in a pet cemetery where his marker reads, "Igloo—He was more than a friend."

Igloo and Richard Byrd during an Antarctic expedition in 1930. National Archives photo no. 306-NT-549A-2

In the 1930s college football was more popular than professional football. The first National Football League (NFL) draft was held in 1936 in Philadelphia, where professional teams congregated to draft the best players from the colleges. Jay Berwanger from the University of Chicago was the first player chosen using the new system. But he ended up not playing professional football at all. Byron White was selected in the first round of the 1938 draft. He played for three years and later became a US Supreme Court Justice.

MUSIC REFLECTS SOCIETY

"INKA DINKA DOO," "Boogie Woogie," "Flat Foot Floogee," and "Dipsy Doodle." If songwriters were trying to create titles that would make people laugh during the Depression Era, most would say they were successful. How could anyone *not* smile at the sound of "Inka Dinka Doo" and "Dipsy Doodle"?

There was plenty of anxiety to go around during the Great Depression, so anything that brought smiles to faces was welcomed. While much of the music of the time was carefree and intended to help Americans relax and have a good time, there was a serious side to the music too.

"Brother, Can You Spare a Dime?" was a popular song that laments the state of affairs in a country where workers had built skyscrapers and railroads and fought a world war but now were standing in breadlines. Woody Guthrie, an Oklahoma Dust Bowl migrant, found a job at a radio station in California where he sang songs he had written about his life on the road. "I Ain't Got No Home," "Goin' Down the Road Feelin' Bad," and "Talking Dust Bowl Blues" told the stories of others like him:

My brothers and my sisters are stranded on this road,
A hot and dusty road that a million feet have trod

And

Back in 1927 I had a little farm . . . rain quit . . . and the black ol' dust storm filled the sky

African American songwriter Huddie Ledbetter, known as Leadbelly, wrote about the impact of the Great Depression on African Americans. His skills on the guitar and his vibrant lyrics at-tracted audiences in white as well as black com-munities. "I couldn't sleep last night . . . the blues walking round my bed . . . I went to eat my break-fast, the blues was in my bread . . ."

Despite the music that recounted the sad times and loss of hope brought on by the Great De-pression, other songs encouraged people to look toward a brighter future. "Old man Depression, you are through . . ." from "We're in the Money"; "The skies above are clear again . . . let's tell the world about it . . ." from "Happy Days Are Here Again"; and "You can't take your dough when you go . . . so live and laugh . . ." from "Life Is Just a Bowl of Cherries."

People were determined to find fun in the gloomy Depression years. And they did—through books and radios, at circuses and mov-ies, and by following their favorite entertainers and sports figures. They were persistent in the hope that happy days would come again. That determination and persistence carried them through the dark days. And when things began to get better, many looked back and recalled hardships—*and* fun times.

HARDSHIP *and* HOPE

The 1930s in America were a time of extreme hardships for many Americans. People who had invested in the stock market lost great sums of money. Banks collapsed, causing people to lose all their savings. Businesses dried up. Unemployment was widespread. Families became homeless. The nation's cities suffered. Farmland blew away. Schools couldn't pay teachers. People were hungry.

Hardship was a big part of life in the 1930s. But the day-to-day lives of Americans held moments of laughter, excitement, anticipation—and most of all hope that things would get better. It was a time when movie stars' pets vacationed on yachts, kids skipped school to attend the circus, and people told jokes about unpopular politicians. Workers struck for higher wages, and although 25 percent of the nation's workers were out of work, 75 percent weren't. Kids looked forward to suppers of pickled pigs' feet. Mothers were excited to get a new flour sack because it meant new underwear for the kids.

The hard times stubbornly hung on into the last year of the decade. In 1939 the economy was still sluggish. Unemployment was still a problem. But in the fall of the year everything changed. Events occurring thousands of miles from America would bring an end to the hardships of the Great Depression.

War had broken out in Europe. And although America was not yet involved in the fighting, the warring nations needed guns, ammunition, planes, food, and clothing. They turned to America, where peoptle were eager to go to work in factories—supplying the world with war materials. It was the beginning of the end of the Great Depression.

THE MYSTERY *of the* MIGRANT FAMILY SOLVED

The stories of the people, places, and events from the past are mysteries waiting to be solved. In 1979 a newspaper reporter in California solved one of the lingering unknowns from the 1930s: What happened to the family in the famous photo—*Migrant Mother*—taken by Dorothea Lange in 1936? And what were the names of the woman and her three little children?

When Dorothea took the picture, she promised the woman she would never reveal her identity. And she never did. She couldn't have—because she never asked the woman's name. But in 1979 a newspaper reporter from the *Modesto Bee* uncovered the names of the woman and her children. They agreed to let him publish their names. Newspapers and television stations eagerly reminded the public of the picture and unraveled the mystery that had remained hidden for so many years.

The *Migrant Mother* was Florence Owens Thompson. She was 75 years old, and the children were now adults. The girl on the left side of the picture is four-year-old Katherine. Ruby is on the right. And the baby is Norma. The family had survived their years as migrant workers.

They talked about their memories. Florence recalled wrapping Norma in a blanket and pulling the bundle as she walked the rows picking cotton. The older children walked ahead in the fields—also picking the crop. Florence had worked at various jobs over the years. She always worked very hard. By 1979 she was retired.

Florence's daughters had some sad memories. It was very difficult to keep clean. They said other kids were cruel at times. They felt ashamed and frightened—that's why the older girls hid their faces from Dorothea Lange's camera. But they had good memories too. They recalled a pet dog. Mostly they praised their mother.

"She was the backbone of our family. She didn't eat sometimes, but she made sure us children ate," Katherine recalled. "We knew she loved us, and that was enough."

She added, "We were proud of her."

And Katherine was no longer ashamed. "We are proud of the story behind the picture."

The experiences of the Thompson family were unique in some ways. Many photos were captured of people who suffered because of the Great Depression. But few received as much attention at the time. And few have left such a lasting impression.

However, as with the Thompson family, people who remember the Great Depression recall sadness and misery. But they also talk about good memories. Almost all believe their lives were forever changed by having lived through one of the toughest times in history.

Katherine McIntosh holds a picture of her mother, herself, and her sisters. Corbis

WEBSITES TO EXPLORE

American Experience.
Surviving the Dust Bowl
www.pbs.org/wgbh/americanexperience
  /films/dustbowl/
Content from the PBS documentary by Ken
Burns. Includes online submissions from
viewers about their memories, archival photos,
articles, transcript of shows, interviews, and
teacher's resources.

The Eleanor Roosevelt Papers Project
www.gwu.edu/~erpapers
Artifacts by and about First Lady Eleanor Roosevelt. Includes teacher resources, archival articles,
"My Day" columns, correspondence, transcripts of
radio programs, and personal papers.

Franklin D. Roosevelt Library and Museum
http://docs.fdrlibrary.marist.edu/gdphotos
  .html
Photos of the Great Depression and New Deal.
Keyword searchable, copyright free.

Library of Congress, Farm
Security Administration
www.loc.gov/pictures/collection/fsa
  /about.html
Photos taken by US government photographers between 1935 and 1944. Includes photos
of slices of life from rural and urban areas.
Famous photographers such as Dorothea
Lange, Carl Mydans, and others are featured.

A New Deal for the Arts
www.archives.gov/exhibits/new_deal_for
  _the_arts/index.html
An online exhibit from the National Archives.
It was originally on display from 1997 to 1998
in the Rotunda of the National Archives Building, Washington, DC. Clustered by subjects
such as "work, activists, and people."

**The Official Site of the Pro
Football Hall of Fame**
www.profootballhof.com/history/general
    /draft/1930s.aspx
Find current NFL information, history, feature stories, photo gallery, and stats.

Old Time Radio
https://archive.org/details/oldtimeradio
Browse and search audio files of old radio programs. Browse by date, subject/keywords, or creator. Includes speeches such as FDR's *Fireside Chats*, children's programs such as *Jerry of the Circus*, serials such as *Vic and Sade*, and musical programming such as Glenn Miller.

Work Projects Administration Posters
www.loc.gov/pictures/collection/wpapos/
Over 900 images publicizing exhibits, community activities, theatrical productions, and health and educational programs sponsored by New Deal programs.

BOOKS

Fiction

Curtis, Christopher Paul. *Bud, Not Buddy*. New York: Laurel Leaf, 2004.

Hesse, Karen. *Out of the Dust*. New York: Scholastic, 2009.

Muñoz Ryan, Pam. *Esperanza Rising*. New York: Scholastic, 2002.

Nonfiction

Burns, Ken, and Dayton Duncan. *The Dust Bowl: An Illustrated History*. San Francisco: Chronicle Books, 2012.

Egan, Timothy. *The Worst Hard Time: The Untold Story of Those Who Survived the Great American Dust Bowl*. New York: Mariner Books, 2006.

Flynn, Kathryn A. *The New Deal: A 75th Anniversary Celebration*. Layton, UT: Gibbs Smith, 2008.

Freedman, Russell. *Children of the Great Depression*. New York: Clarion, 2005.

Gay, Georgia Lee. *Whatever Happened to MacNolia Cox?* Baltimore: Publish America, 2008.

Panchyk, Richard. *Franklin Delano Roosevelt for Kids*. Chicago: Chicago Review Press, 2007.

Stanley, Jerry. *Children of the Dust Bowl: The True Story of the School at Weedpatch Camp*. New York: Crown, 1993.

NOTES

CHAPTER 1:
The 1920s: Roaring Toward a Crash

Robert Tyre Jones Jr. was competing: Cooke, *Alistair Cooke's America*, 322.

The decade of the 1920s was known: McElvaine, *The Great Depression: America, 1929–1941*, 13.

In Michigan eight-year-old Charles: New York Times, January 22, 1922.

"Food will win the war": Schwieder, *Iowa: The Middle Land*, 148.

One man joked that his wife: Chicago Daily Tribune, May 13, 1928.

There was a nurse who made: Ellis, *A Nation in Torment: The Great American Depression, 1929–1939*, 31.

"you policemen may protect them": New York Times, August 14, 1921.

In Indiana a group of citizens drove: New York Times, June 12, 1921.

The New York Times *reported that officials at the Naval Academy: New York Times*, April 9, 1922.

In 1900, 90 percent of African Americans: Isabel Wilkerson, interview, NPR, September 13, 2010.

"I liked him okay": Rollins, *All Is Never Said: The Narrative of Odette Harper Hines*, 47.

It was her mother's encouragement: Carney Smith, *Notable Black American Women*, 544.

Young men in the 1920s wore: Drowne and Huber, *The 1920s*, 111.

When one partner got so tired: Telephone interview with Vivian DuShane, January 24, 2014.

Indians' Dances Shock Morals of Mr. Burke: Chicago Daily Tribune, May 10, 1921.

In 1919 there were only 7 million: McElvaine, *The Great Depression: America, 1929–41*, 18.

In 1914 a Ford car cost: Alistair Cooke's *America*, 317.

When historians looked back: Klein, *Rainbow's End: The Crash of 1929*, 8.

CHAPTER 2: *America Looks to Its Leaders for Help*

When the stock market crashed in 1929: Digital History: *The Human Toll.* www.digitalhistory.uh.edu/disp_textbook.cfm?smtID=2&psid=3434.

Every veteran who had served overseas was promised: Watkins, *The Hungry Years: A Narrative History of the Great Depression*, 132.

When a soldier used his bayonet to jab: Terkel, *Hard Times*, 16.

According to news reports, police picked up: "Police Clubs Rout Hunger Marchers," *Daily Boston Globe*, October 31, 1934.

In New Jersey, children played games: "The Siege Is Ended," *Washington Post*, May 3, 1936.

Two-month-old Bernard Myers: "Bonus Marcher's Infant Son Dies at Gallinger," *Washington Post*, August 10, 1932.

CHAPTER 3: *Broken Cities and Breadlines—Urban Life*

In Detroit men determined to be first in line: Manchester, *The Glory and the Dream*, 40.

In 1931 New York City was serving 85,000: Watkins, *The Hungry Years*, 59.

In Seattle 450: Edsforth, *The New Deal: America's Response to the Great Depression*, 95.

"I was paid until June 1931…": Terkel, *Hard Times*, 388.

"Never in the history of this country": "Tugwell Town May Pay Out in 237 Long Years," *Chicago Daily Tribune*, September 3, 1937.

A news reporter who visited the school: "Greenbelt Pupils Find Conservation a Route to Education," *Washington Post*, March 26, 1939.

"A wonderland where": "Enchanted Island" Special Collections Research Center, University of Chicago Library. Call No. Crerar Ms. 226 v. 5 no. 50, www.lib.uchicago.edu/cgi-bin/nand/search/century?layout=longlayout&rec=0+100094%3A128

CHAPTER 4:
Droughts, Dust Storms, and Pest Plagues—Rural Life

"They came mysteriously": "Fields Denuded by Grasshoppers," *Daily Boston Globe*, July 28, 1931.

Communities along the path of the flood: National Weather Service Weather Forecast Office, "Republican River Flood of May 30, 1935." www.crh.noaa.gov/gld/?n=1935flood.

More than 4,000 farm and town: "Massive 1930s Floods Ravaged Colorado River Basin," *Johnson City Record Courier*, July 8, 2010. www.jcrecordcourier.com/news/32150/.

"Endless miles of usually rich": "Calamity May Soon Rival the Depression," *Washington Post*, August 12, 1934.

"The dust piled to the top": "His Farm Now Ocean of Dirt," *Daily Boston Globe*, April 14, 1935.

"The big field looks": Ibid.

He had no idea what lay ahead: "Young Kansan Lost All Night in Dust Storm," *Washington Post*, April 14, 1935.

"My farm moved out": "A Measure of Recovery," *Ken Magazine*, June 2, 1938.

"Cotton pickin' season's": "A Measure of Recovery," *Ken Magazine*, June 2, 1938.

Farmers were right: Manchester, *The Glory and the Dream*, 42.

In September 1935 Eleanor Waters: "The Montgomery Farm Women's Cooperative Market," *The Montgomery County Story*, vol. 25, no. 3, August 1982.

Because farmers were getting such terrible prices: Schwieder, *Iowa: The Middle Land*, 265.

In Georgia experts estimated: "Women to the Rescue," *Washington Post*, February 10, 1933.

In 1933 North Carolina: "4-H and Home Demonstration During the Great Depression," *North Carolina Digital History*. www.learnnc .org/lp/editions/nchist-worldwar/1332.

These reports of the contributions of farm women: "Heroic Farm Women," *Washington Post*, August 14, 1933.

In 1935 there were 6.8 million farmers: Zinn, *A Young People's History of the United States*, 289.

In 1930, of the 835,000 black men: Watkins, *The Hungry Years*, 373.

The tenants and sharecroppers lived in houses: Watkins, *The Hungry Years*, 374.

In the late 1930s Lula Wright: "A Day with Lula Wright," University of North Carolina University Libraries, The Southern Historical Collection, Folder 59: Perry, Rhussus L. http://dc.lib.unc.edu/cdm/ref/collection /03709/id/993.

CHAPTER 5:
Growing Up in Tough Times

Patience Abbe was 12 years: "Patience Abbe, Chronicler of Her Childhood Travels, Dies at 87," *New York Times*, March 31, 2012.

"Dad lost his job": Minehan, *Boy and Girl Tramps of America.* http://xroads.virginia.edu /~ma01/white/anthology/tramps.html.

"A country school offers": "Boys and Girls Fitted For Life," *Los Angeles Times*, August 27, 1933.

"[S]chool histories . . . we do know": LaPier and Beck, "Crossroads for a Culture," *Chicago History*, 37.

One textbook had this to say: Ward, *History in the Making: An Absorbing Look at How American History Has Changed in the Telling over the Last 200 Years*, 13.

The winner that year was Jean Trowbridge: "Dictionary Saves Queen of Spellers," *The Gazette*, June 26, 1936.

Some people believed that the word "nemesis": Telephone interview with Naomi Turman, May 10, 2014.

The word "nemesis" means: Merriam-Webster. www.merriam-webster.com/dictionary /nemesis.

Established in June 1935: Watkins, *The Hungry Years*, 270.

In 1934 a teacher at Public School 36: "Her Generosity Snags Teacher," *Brooklyn Daily Eagle*, August 13, 1934.

"I never knew there were so many different ways to serve . . .": "Don't Let the Children Know," *Daily Boston Globe*, November 13, 1932.

In Boston, Massachusetts, schoolkids were lucky: "Feeding Depression's Children," *Daily Boston Globe*, May 29, 1932.

"It is common to see children": "Teeth of Children Injured by Depression," *Los Angeles Times*, March 14, 1937.

"For the past seven or eight years": "Teeth of Children Injured by Depression," *Daily Boston Globe*, March 14, 1937.

In 1934 a survey conducted by the Society for the Prevention of: "More Child Neglect in '33 than in '29," *Daily Boston Globe*, March 4, 1934.

Researchers at the University of Vermont: "Children Found Healthier in Cities than on Farms; Blame Cut Incomes," *Daily Boston Globe*, April 23, 1939.

Donald B. Willard, a reporter: "'Cheese It, Baby Hippo, The Moose!' Is Modern Boston Schoolboy Slang," *Daily Boston Globe*, May 18, 1930.

"We didn't realize we were doing without": The People in the Pictures: Stories from the Wettach Farm Photos. www.iptv.org/iowastories/detail.cfm/wettach.

One dad proudly recalled: "Don't Let the Children Know," *Daily Boston Globe*, November 13, 1932.

CHAPTER 6: *Helping Hands and a "New Deal" Awaken Hope*

Each one was a little different: History Magazine, February/March 2008.

In fact, that was exactly what Mrs. Roosevelt envisioned: "Mrs. Roosevelt Finds CCC for Idle Women Is a Good Thing," *Chicago Daily Tribune*, October 23, 1934.

The Daily Boston Globe *caught the attention of readers:* "Schools for Maids to Cost $500,000," *Daily Boston Globe*, February 16, 1936.

"It is necessary that the Indians themselves": "Indians Call for Full Citizenship; Resent Being Wards," *Chicago Daily Tribune*, September 28, 1929.

CHAPTER 7: *Finding Fun in Gloomy Times*

The mayor, Andrew J. Gillis, also known: "Children Go to Circus, but Attend School First Despite Gillis Edict," *Daily Boston Globe*, May 30, 1931.

In 1930, 12 million households had radios: History Detectives. www.pbs.org/opb/historydetectives/feature/radio-in-the-1930s/.

In 1932 over half the population: Manchester, The Glory and the Dream, 38.

"as a means of weathering the current financial storm.": "Movie Stars Accept Cuts to Help Meet Bank Crisis," *Daily Boston Globe*, March 9, 1933.

In the May 1938 issue: "Mouth-Moving Mouthings," *Double Talk*, May 5, 1938.

"I'd just as soon have her be a": "Seven-Year-Old Girl is Adept at Stage Magic," *Ogden Standard-Examiner*, June 19, 1930.

Dorothy DeBorba was only five years old: Our Gang Online. www.ramseyltd.com/rascals /dorothy/.

In an interview he admitted: "'Badest' Robber Is Killed Twice," *Daily Boston Globe*, November 6, 1938.

An editorial in the New York Times*:* Thornton, "New Yorkers Deserve More Funding for Libraries." www.nypl.org/blog/2009/03/11 /open-doors-open-minds-new-york-public -library-during-great-depression-and-today %E2%80%99s-ec.

On April 2, as the legendary Babe Ruth: Smithsonian, July–August, 2013.

On the train trip to Los Angeles: Research Quarterly for Exercise and Sport, June 1, 1996.

Tidye made history: Stout, *Yes, She Can!: Women's Sports Pioneers*, 59.

The first National Football League (NFL) draft: "Pro Football Draft History: The 1930s," The Official Site of the Pro Football Hall of Fame. www.profootballhof.com/history/general/draft /1930s.aspx.

POSTSCRIPT:
The Mystery of the Migrant Family Solved

"She was the backbone of our family ...": CNN.com. www.cnn.com/2008/LIVING/12 /02/dustbowl.photo/index.html?iref=allsearch.

"We were proud of her.": SFGate.com. www.sfgate.com/default/article/Daughter-of -Migrant-Mother-proud-of-story-3221049.php.

BIBLIOGRAPHY

☞ Suitable for younger readers

BOOKS

☞ Bollow, Ludmilla. *Lulu's Christmas Story: A True Story of Faith and Hope During the Great Depression*. New York: Titletown Publishing, 2014.

☞ Burgan, Michael. *The Great Depression*. North Mankato, MN: Capstone Press, 2011.

Carney Smith, Jessie, ed. *Notable Black American Women*. Detroit: Gale Research, 1992.

Cooke, Alistair. *Alistair Cooke's America*. New York: Alfred A. Knopf, 1974.

Drowne, Kathleen, and Patrick Huber. *The 1920s*. Westport, CT: Greenwood Press, 2004.

Dunning, John. *On the Air: The Encyclopedia of Old-Time Radio*. New York: Oxford University Press, 1998.

Edsforth, Ronald. *The New Deal: America's Response to the Great Depression*. Malden, MA: Blackwell Publishers, 2000.

Ellis, Edward Robb. *A Nation in Torment: The Great American Depression, 1929–1939*. New York: Kodansha International, 1995.

☞ Freedman, Russell. *Children of the Great Depression*. New York: Houghton Mifflin Harcourt, 2005.

Klein, Maury. *Rainbow's End: The Crash of 1929*. New York: Oxford University Press, 2003.

Knepper, Cathy D. *Greenbelt, Maryland: A Living Legacy of the New Deal*. Baltimore: Johns Hopkins University Press, 2001.

Manchester, William. *The Glory and the Dream*. Boston: Little, Brown and Company, 1974.

McElvaine, Robert. *The Great Depression: America, 1929–1941*. New York: Three Rivers Press, 2009.

☞ Minehan, Thomas. *Boy and Girl Tramps of America*. New York: Grosset, 1934.

☞ Nardo, Don, Alexa L. Sandmann, and Kathleen Baxter. *Migrant Mother: How a Photograph Defined the Great Depression*. Mankato, MN: Compass Point Books, 2011.

☞ Panchyk, Richard. *Franklin Delano Roosevelt for Kids*. Chicago: Chicago Review Press, 2007.

Rollins, Judith. *All Is Never Said: The Narrative of Odette Harper Hines*. Philadelphia: Temple University Press, 1995.

Schwieder, Dorothy. *Iowa: The Middle Land*. Ames: Iowa State University Press, 1996.

Shlaes, Amity. *The Forgotten Man: A New History of the Great Depression*. New York: Harper, 2007.

Sterling, Christopher H., and Cary O'Dell, eds. *The Concise Encyclopedia of American Radio*. New York: Routledge, 2009.

Stout, Glenn. *Yes, She Can!: Women's Sports Pioneers*. Boston: Houghton Mifflin Harcourt, 2011.

Terkel, Studs. *Hard Times*. New York: The New Press, 1986.

Ward, Kyle. *History in the Making: An Absorbing Look at How American History Has Changed in the Telling over the Last 200 Years*. New York: The New Press, 2006.

Watkins, T. H. *The Hungry Years: A Narrative History of the Great Depression in America*. New York: Henry Holt and Company, 1999.

Wenger, Tisa. *We Have a Religion: The 1920s Pueblo Indian Dance Controversy and American Religious Freedom*. Chapel Hill: University of North Carolina Press, 2009.

Wilkerson, Isabel. *The Warmth of Other Suns: The Epic Story of America's Great Migration*. New York: Random House, 2011.

☞ Zinn, Howard. *A Young People's History of the United States*. New York: Seven Stories Press, 2007.

INTERVIEWS

Telephone interview with Vivian DuShane, January 24, 2014.

Telephone interview with Naomi Turman, May 10, 2014.

JOURNALS

Himes Gissendanner, Cindy. "African American Women Olympians: The Impact of Race, Gender, and Class Ideologies, 1932–1968." *Research Quarterly for Exercise and Sport*, June 1, 1996.

MAGAZINES

Crook, Mary Charlotte. "The Montgomery Farm Women's Cooperative Market." *The Montgomery County Story*, August 1982.

Horwitz, Tony. "League of Her Own." *Smithsonian*, July–August 2013.

Kahramanidis, Jane. "The She-She-She Camps of the Great Depression." *History Magazine*, February/March 2008.

Koontz, Chucky. "Mouth-Moving Mouthings." *Double Talk*, May 1938.

LaPier, Rosalyn R., and David R. M. Beck. "Crossroads for a Culture." *Chicago History: The Magazine of the Chicago History Museum*, Spring 2012.

"A Measure of Recovery." *Ken Magazine*, June 2, 1938.

Robertson, William F. "A Troop Treasure Hunt." Boy Scouts of America. *Scouting* 22, no. 1, January 1934. http://texashistory.unt.edu/ark:/67531/metapth312991. University of North Texas Libraries, The Portal to Texas History. Crediting Boy Scouts of America National Scouting Museum, Irving, Texas.

NEWSPAPERS

"Admiral Byrd's Pet Dog Is Dead, Lectures Cancelled." *Free Lance Star*, April 21, 1931.

"Al Attends a Wet Party." *Chicago Daily Tribune*, May 13, 1928.

"'Badest' Robber Is Killed Twice." *Daily Boston Globe*, November 6, 1938.

"Best Speller Stumbles over Word Nemesis." *Afro American*, May 30, 1936.

"Bonus Marcher's Infant Son Dies at Gallinger." *Washington Post*, August 10, 1932.

"Calamity May Soon Rival the Depression." *Washington Post*, August 12, 1934.

"'Cheese It, Baby Hippo, The Moose!' Is Modern Boston Schoolboy Slang." *Daily Boston Globe*, May 18, 1930.

"Children Found Healthier in Cities than on Farms; Blame Cut Incomes." *Daily Boston Globe*, April 23, 1939.

"Children Go to Circus, but Attend School First Despite Gillis Edict." *Daily Boston Globe*, May 30, 1931.

"Children Make Unique Contribution to Art Show." *Chicago Defender*, November 12, 1938.

"Dictionary Saves Queen of Spellers." *The Gazette*, June 26, 1936.

"Domestics in Strike Threat." *Spokane Press*, November 5, 1937.

"Don't Let the Children Know." *Daily Boston Globe*, November 13, 1932.

"Efficiency Expert Turned Loose on Hollywood." *Daily Boston Globe*, January 3, 1932.

"Feeding Depression's Children." *Daily Boston Globe*, May 29, 1932.

"Fields Denuded by Grasshoppers." *Daily Boston Globe*, July 28, 1931.

"Greenbelt Pupils Find Conservation a Route to Education." *Washington Post*, March 26, 1939.

"Her Generosity Snags Teacher." *Brooklyn Daily Eagle*, August 13, 1934.

"Heroic Farm Women." *Washington Post*, August 14, 1933.

"His Farm Now Ocean of Dirt." *Daily Boston Globe*, April 14, 1935.

"Indians Call for Full Citizenship; Resent Being Wards." *Chicago Daily Tribune*, September 28, 1929.

"Indians' Dances Shock Morals of Mr. Burke." *Chicago Daily Tribune*, May 10, 1921.

"Massive 1930s Floods Ravaged Colorado River Basin." www.jcrecordcourier.com/news/32150/.

"Meals for Children Continued." *Los Angeles Times*, December 13, 1931.

"Miners Drive Out Aliens." *New York Times*, June 12, 1921.

"More Child Neglect in '33 than in '29," *Daily Boston Globe*, March 4, 1934.

"Movie Stars Accept Cuts to Help Meet Bank Crisis." *Daily Boston Globe*, March 9, 1933.

"Mrs. Roosevelt Finds CCC for Idle Women Is a Good Thing." *Chicago Daily Tribune*, October 23, 1934.

"Negro Cadet Issue." *New York Times*, April 9, 1922.

"Overall Clubs Spread in All Parts of Nation." *New York Times*, April 1, 1920.

"The Overworked Farm Child." *New York Times*, January 22, 1922.

"Patience Abbe, Chronicler of Her Childhood Travels, Dies at 87." *New York Times*, March 31, 2012.

"Police Clubs Rout Hunger Marchers." *Daily Boston Globe*, October 31, 1934.

"Schools for Maids to Cost $500,000." *Daily Boston Globe*, February 16, 1936.

"The Siege Is Ended." *Washington Post*, May 3, 1936.

"Start Foreigners' Exodus." *New York Times*, July 14, 1921.

"Teeth of Children Injured by Depression." *Los Angeles Times*, March 14, 1937.

"Tugwell Town May Pay Out in 237 Long Years." *Chicago Daily Tribune*, September 3, 1937.

"Women to the Rescue." *Washington Post*, February 10, 1933.

"Young Kansan Lost All Night in Dust Storm." *Washington Post*, April 14, 1935.

REPORTS

Meriam, Lewis. "The Problem of Indian Administration." Baltimore: Johns Hopkins University Press, 1928. http://files.eric.ed.gov/fulltext/ED087573.pdf.

THESES

Dunlop, Chelsea Rae. "American Dance Marathons, 1928–1934, and the Social Drama and Ritual Process." Florida State University, 2006. http://diginole.lib.fsu.edu/cgi/viewcontent.cgi?article=1358&context=etd.

VIDEO

"Interview with Florence Thompson, the Mona Lisa of the Dust Bowl." *NBC Today Show*, New York: NBC Universal, October 30, 1979. NBC Learn. https://archives.nbclearn.com/portal/site/k-12/browse/?cuecard=1526 (accessed September 5, 2012).

The People in the Pictures: Stories from the Wettach Farm Photos. Iowa Public Television. http://www.iptv.org/iowastories/detail.cfm/wettach.

"Radio in the 1930s." *History Detectives.* www.pbs.org/opb/historydetectives/feature /radio-in-the-1930s/.

WEBSITES

"A Day with Lula Wright." UNC, The Southern Historical Collection, Federal Writers' Project papers. http://dc.lib.unc.edu/cdm/ref /collection/03709/id/993.

Digital History, Textbook, 1930s. www.digital history.uh.edu/era.cfm?eraID=14&smtID=2.

"Girl from Iconic Great Depression Photo: 'We were ashamed.'" http://www.cnn.com/2008 /LIVING/12/02/dustbowl.photo/index.html ?iref=allsearch.

Jones, Carolyn. "Daughter of 'Migrant Mother' Proud of Story." SFGate.com. www.sfgate .com/default/article/Daughter-of-Migrant -Mother-proud-of-story-3221049.php.

Manor, Amy. "4-H and Home Demonstration During the Great Depression." *North Carolina Digital History.* www.learnnc.org/lp/editions /nchist-worldwar/1332.

The Official Site of the Pro Football Hall of Fame. www.profootballhof.com/history /general/draft/1930s.aspx.

Our Gang Online. http://www.ramseyltd.com /rascals/dorothy/.

"Republican River Flood of May 30, 1935." National Weather Service Weather Forecast Office. www.crh.noaa.gov/gld/?n=1935flood.

Thornton, Ann. "Open Doors, Open Minds: The New York Public Library During the Great Depression and Today's Economic Crisis." March 11, 2009. www.nypl.org/blog/2009/03 /11/open-doors-open-minds-new-york-public -library-during-great-depression-and-today %E2%80%99s-ec.

INDEX

Page numbers in *italics* indicate pictures